Praise for *Gender and the Nicene Creed*
by Elizabeth Rankin Geitz

"Elizabeth Geitz has done a beautiful job in recovering that which has been lost and found and lost again and again—feminine attributes of God and some important feminine traditions of Christianity. I, for one, am gratefully in her debt."

The Rev. William Sloane Coffin
Former Pastor, Riverside Church, New York, N.Y.
author of A Passion for the Possible

"Conventional notions of meaning and gender are challenged, horizons are broadened, and wider perspectives are offered by the solid research and careful reasoning upon which this study is based. Anyone who is seriously considering the Christian creedal tradition, its foundations in the Bible and early church as well as its problems for today's thought world, will need to read this book before a responsible conclusion can be formed."

The Rev. Canon J. Robert Wright, Ph.D.
St. Mark's Professor of Ecclesiastical History
General Theological Seminary, New York, N.Y.

"I recommend Geitz' work both for learning and for a not-so-gentle nudge to live what we profess in the Nicene Creed to believe."

Jane Holmes Dixon
Suffragan Bishop of Washington

"Knowing that tradition need never be static, Elizabeth Rankin Geitz probes and challenges the language of the Nicene Creed and Trinitarian theology. Thoughtfully exploring words and images in light of her own experience and reading, she widens understanding and offers more inclusive approaches to faith and worship. Women and men will draw encouragement and new insight from this fine study

The Rt. Rev. Fre
Bishop of the Di

T0165924

i

". . . a brave attempt to take discussion of the creed out of the hands of theologians and academics and turn it over to ordinary Christians. A good introduction to alternative theological positions, it blends careful scholarship with experiential and sermonic materials in an interesting and engaging way."

The Rev. Suzanne R. Hiatt, L.L.D.
Professor of Pastoral Theology
Episcopal Divinity School, Cambridge, Mass.

"This book will make those who insist on exclusively patriarchal claims about God very uncomfortable, for they will find their point of view countered both in Scripture and in the writings of the early church fathers, leading mystics, and revered saints. Examining the Nicene Creed, the foundational creed of orthodox theology, it becomes increasingly clear to the reader that God is beyond gender specificity, but also that our worship and our theology are enhanced in the use of the rich feminine imagery found in our Christian tradition."

The Rt. Rev Joe Morris Doss
Bishop of the Diocese of New Jersey

"Geitz' blend of traditional Christian belief and piety with feminist convictions is an eye-opener. Especially for the many dedicated church people who question whether Christian faith and feminism can live happily and honestly together, her work is a great help. Geitz is a good guide for all who want to live the fullness of Christian faith as twentieth-century women."

The Rev. Patricia Wilson-Kastner, Ph.D.
author of Faith, Feminism, and the Christ

"*Gender and the Nicene Creed* stays within the parameters of the historic faith . . . is theologically sound . . . mediating in tone, irenic in spirit . . . quite accessible and readable . . . distinctive within its genre. I know of no such other book."

Timothy Sedgwick, Ph.D.
Professor, of Church Ethics and Moral Theology
Seabury-Western Theological Seminary, Evanston, Ill.

GENDER AND THE
NICENE CREED

ELIZABETH RANKIN GEITZ

Church Publishing
NEW YORK

A catalog record for this book is available from the Library of Congress.

ISBN: 978-0-89869-471-0

Church Publishing, Incorporated.
445 Fifth Avenue
New York, New York 10016
Printed in the United States of America

www.churchpublishing.org

To Charlotte, my daughter
To the memory of Dorothy Ann, my mother
and Elizabeth and Mary Frances, my grandmothers
with admiration, love, and gratitude
for all they have been and will become

OTHER BOOKS BY
ELIZABETH RANKIN GEITZ

Entertaining Angels

Welcoming the Stranger

Recovering Lost Tradition
(with Margaret Hayes Prescott)

CONTENTS

ACKNOWLEDGMENTS

My deep appreciation goes to the Rev. Dr. J. Robert Wright, my mentor throughout the writing of this book. His scholarly knowledge, expertise, insight, and encouragement have been invaluable to me. His gentle corrections and proddings have enabled me to offer a book to the Christian community that is both theologically and historically sound and one that we hope will be utilized in future ecumenical dialogue regarding the Nicene Creed.

My further thanks goes to the Rev. Dr. Patricia Wilson-Kastner and the Rev. Dr. Clarice Martin whose suggestions regarding the manuscript enabled me to include material that became central to it.

As always, I thank my husband, Michael, for his continued, unfailing support of my work; and my children, Charlotte, and Michael R., who remind me daily of what the love of God is all about.

Grateful acknowledgment is made to the following publishers for permission to use the works cited:

Excerpts from the writings of Dorothy L. Sayers reprinted by permission of the author and the Watkins/Loomis Agency.

The Medical Mission Sisters for permission to reproduce "You Shall Be My Witnesses," words and music by Miriam Therese Winter, ©1987.

Paulist Press, for permission to quote from three publications: *Spiritual Friend,* Tilden Edwards, ©1980, p. 139; *Silent Voices, Sacred Lives,* Barbara Bowe et al., ©1992, pp. 52-53; and *Women at the Well,* Kathleen Fischer, ©1988, p. 81.

Maracelle Thiebaux, for permission to quote from *The Writings of Medieval Women,* Trans., ©1987, pp. 143-144.

PREFACE

One Sunday morning I was suddenly jolted out of my pew. In the middle of a sermon, the preacher referred to God as "she." At first I thought I had heard her incorrectly; then she said it again. I rolled my eyes around to the woman sitting next to me, as if to say, "What is this?" With a knowing look on her face, my friend leaned over and whispered in my ear, "She's from California."

With complete understanding, I nodded. "That explains it," I thought. "This is an outgrowth of the women's movement." I decided it was all right for my priest to call God "she" if it made her feel better, and I did not focus on it further.

Then in the late 1980s the Episcopal Church began experimenting with an inclusive-language liturgy for its service of Holy Communion. Not only was language about men and women made inclusive, God-language became gender neutral as well. This was going too far. Sermon references were one thing; creating another liturgy for the church was quite another.

In the midst of these changes, I felt called to the priesthood, was made a postulant in the Diocese of New Jersey, and began attending seminary. During the spring semester of my first year, Margaret Prescott, a classmate, asked me to work on a project with her relating to the Supplemental Liturgical Texts, the proposed inclusive-language liturgy of the Episcopal Church. My stomach knotted up. I had no desire to spend significant amounts of time on such a project. I wasn't oppressed! What were these women angry about anyway?

Fortunately, Margaret persuaded me to look beyond my surface emotions and do some serious research. What were the historical and theological reasons for the liturgy? Was there such a basis for the texts, or was it merely an outgrowth of contemporary concerns?

After months of research, I gradually realized how wrong I had been. There *were* sound scriptural, theological, and historical reasons for the proposed liturgy. Why had I never been exposed to the teachings of the church that I was uncovering? Why had a significant part of the Christian tradition been completely ignored?

At this point, Margaret and I self-published our work on the supplemental liturgies, *Recovering Lost Tradition*. Since that time, I have been committed to educating others in the lost traditions of our church. My desire is to help us move from an initial emotional response to feminine traditions of the church, to one that is based on sound biblical, historical, and theological principles. As committed Christians, isn't this what God requires of us, lay and clergy alike? If we truly care about the future of our church in these times of transition, it is our responsibility to educate ourselves as best we can, so we can make informed personal and corporate decisions.

After working on the language issue with regard to the liturgy, I found myself filled with questions. I was troubled by what my research had uncovered and I was not sure how my resulting theology meshed with the orthodoxy of the church.

While continuing my studies for the priesthood at General Theological Seminary, I was asked to write a series of papers stating what the Nicene Creed meant to me. I was concerned. Was the orthodoxy of the Nicene Creed, completed in the year 381, still relevant to my faith?

In answering this question, I first had to look at the definition of orthodoxy. Contrary to what I thought, orthodoxy is not stagnant, never-changing, and set for all time by the early church writers. A correct understanding of orthodoxy arises from a correct understanding of the nature of God and God's relationship to the created world. Just as God revealed Godself to the Israelites, so God's self-revelation continues today. Thus, God's participation in the history of humankind, salvation history, was and is and always will be.

Just as the understanding of God is not frozen in time, neither should the church's understanding of Jesus be fixed for all time. Eduard Schweizer wrote: "The church must continue to make fresh statements of who Jesus is. It can never reduce these statements to a single final formula that would define Jesus for the rest of time."[1]

Throughout the tradition of our church, numerous theologians have made fresh statements about God, Jesus, and the Holy Spirit. Yet, predominantly only one strand of the tradition has been taught, the strand that elucidates a patriarchal perspective. Whereas this strand is indeed the dominant one, it is not the only one. Running alongside the patriarchal tradition is another that is rich in feminine imagery, expanding the images for God, Jesus and the Holy Spirit to reflect theologically that God, and therefore the Trinity, is eternally and essentially beyond gender specificity.[2]

When self-proclaimed church "traditionalists" choose to define tradition selectively as only part of the tradition of our church, I am concerned; for such selectivity is not only disheartening, but also unfaithful to what the full, rich tradition of our church actually includes. It is this lost tradition that I seek to recover. Recovering and recapturing lost tradition is what I am suggesting, not creating something out of whole cloth to answer only a twentieth-century concern.

In addition, it is this lost tradition that enables me to find my theology within the hallowed tradition of our church. I thank God for giving me the tools and the support of many fine scholars who have helped me see myself in the words and reflections of theologians, mystics, and scholars throughout the centuries.

I could never say that the part of our tradition that speaks to me should be definitive for all Christians. Likewise, the part of the tradition that speaks to someone else may or may not be definitive for me. For just as we have a pluralistic canon for a reason, I believe we have a pluralistic tradition for a reason also. God has spoken to different people in different ways throughout the history of our church. God continues to speak to different people in different ways today.

My offering here is meant to be one voice among others who may also be valid and true to our tradition. It is important to state that for some voices, perhaps many voices, to be valid and true, there must be some who are not. I am not advocating a limitless diversity with no boundaries. There are boundaries. What I am advocating is that a fair hearing be accorded to those who feel called to respond to a part of our tradition that has been ignored for centuries by the church.

Gender and the Nicene Creed is meant to be one thread in a richly woven tapestry that needs others to complete the picture. This one thread that is reflective of my theology contains the insights of classical, neo-orthodox, Eastern, Anglican, Catholic, Protestant, Black, Asian, Latin American, feminist, and womanist[2] theologians.

I offer my reflections on the Nicene Creed, based on the authority of scripture, tradition, and reason, as an invitation to you to do the same. Only when I can join my insights with women and men from all races and ethnic groups from all parts of God's creation will my own understanding of the richness of the Nicene Creed be enhanced.

In *The School of Charity: Meditations on the Christian Creed*, Evelyn Underhill states that the creeds' "chief gift to us, their average brothers and sisters, does not consist in the production of striking spiritual novelties, but rather in the penetrating light which they cast on the familiar truths of religion; showing us that these truths are many-levelled, and will only yield up their unspeakable richness and beauty to those who take the trouble to dig below the surface, and seek for the Treasure which is still hidden in the field."[3]

Digging below the surface of commonly held understandings of the Nicene Creed has yielded innumerable treasures. Perhaps by sharing the insights gleaned from my efforts, you will be encouraged to work further in this rich field God has planted for us all.

Elizabeth

TRANSLATIONS OF THE NICENE CREED

Before exploring the Nicene Creed in depth, a word about the different English translations of the creed is in order. The most widely used English translation of the Nicene Creed today is that of the International Consultation on English Texts or ICET translation. This version was published in 1975 and contains several mistranslations of the original Greek text.

By comparing the original Greek translation of the creed with the ICET version, on pages 6 and 7, you will note that there are several significant differences. First, "and the Son" (line 27) is not in the original Greek text. Second, "he became incarnate *from* the Virgin Mary" (line 16) was, in the original Greek, "was incarnate of the Holy Spirit *and* the Virgin Mary," emphasizing Mary's active rather than passive role in the incarnation. Line 16 will be discussed further in chapter VI.

In addition, the pronoun "he" in relation to the Holy Spirit, found in the ICET translation, is also absent from the original Greek text. There are no gender-restrictive articles in the Greek text related to the Holy Spirit; rather, they are neuter. The ICET version of the Nicene Creed is used in the *1979 Book of Common Prayer*. A more in-depth discussion of these differences is included in chapter IX.

A more accurate translation of the Nicene Creed is the English Language Liturgical Consultation (ELLC) translation. The Consultation was formed in 1985. As you can see from the text itself, on page 8, it is a more accurate translation of the original Greek. This is the translation used in the Supplemental Liturgical Materials of the Episcopal Church.

Throughout the text of this book, these two different translations of the Nicene Creed will be referred to as ICET and ELLC.

The Nicene Creed (Literal Translation of the Original Greek)

We believe in one God, the Father, the almighty,
    maker of heaven and earth,
    of all things visible and invisible.

And in one Lord Jesus Christ,
    the only-begotten Son of God, begotten from the Father
    before all ages, light from light, true God from true God,
    begotten not made, of one substance with the Father,
    through whom all things came into existence,
    who because of us **humans** and because of our salvation
    came down from heaven, and was incarnate
    of the Holy Spirit **and** the Virgin Mary and became **human**,
    and was crucified for us under Pontius Pilate,
    and suffered and was buried, and rose again on the third day
    according to the Scriptures and ascended to heaven,
    and sits on the right hand of the Father, and will come again
    with glory to judge living and dead,
    of whose kingdom there will be no end;

And in the Holy Spirit, the Lord and life-giver,
    who proceeds from the Father, **who** with the Father and the Son
    is together worshipped and together glorified,
    who spoke through the prophets; in one holy Catholic and
    apostolic Church. We confess one baptism to the remission of sins;
    we look forward to the resurrection of the dead
    and the life of the world to come. Amen.

*Note the correct translation of the Greek word "anthropos" as "human,"
the relation of the Holy Spirit and the Virgin Mary, and the consistent
neuter article "who" in reference to the Holy Spirit.*

The Nicene Creed (ICET Translation)

We believe in one God,
    the Father, the Almighty,
    maker of heaven and earth,
    of all that is, seen and unseen.

We believe in one Lord, Jesus Christ,
    the only Son of God,
    eternally begotten of the Father,
    God from God, Light from Light,
    true God from true God,
    begotten, not made,
    of one Being with the Father.
    Through him all things were made.
    For us and for our salvation
        he came down from heaven:
    by the power of the Holy Spirit
        he became incarnate from the Virgin Mary,
        and was made **man**.
    For our sake he was crucified under Pontius Pilate;
        he suffered death and was buried.
        On the third day he rose again
            in accordance with the Scriptures;
        he ascended into heaven
            and is seated at the right hand of the Father.
    He will come again in glory to judge the living and the dead,
        and his kingdom will have no end.

We believe in the Holy Spirit, the Lord, the giver of life,
    who proceeds from the Father **and the Son**.
    With the Father and the Son **he** is worshiped and glorified.
    He has spoken through the Prophets.
    We believe in one holy catholic and apostolic Church.
    We acknowledge one baptism for the forgiveness of sins.
    We look for the resurrection of the dead,
        and the life of the world to come. Amen.

*This is the International Consultation on English Texts (ICET) transla-
tion. The texts were published in final form in 1975 in* Prayers We Have
in Common. *This is the version used in the 1979 Book of Common
Prayer. Note the incorrect translations in lines 16, 17, 27, 28, 29. This
is due, in part, to the fact that versions of the creed contained in the
Prayer Books of 1549 up until the current 1979 book were translated
from the Latin of Dionysus Exiguus (500 - 550) and not from the text
given in the Greek Acta of the Council of Chalcedon, which is the
source of the original text.*

The Nicene Creed (ELLC Translation)

We believe in one God,
   the Father, the Almighty,
   maker of heaven and earth,
   of all that is, seen and unseen.

We believe in one Lord, Jesus Christ,
   the only Son of God,
   eternally begotten of the Father,
   God from God, Light from Light,
   true God from true God,
   begotten, not made,
   of one Being with the Father;
   through him all things were made.
   For us and for our salvation
      he came down from heaven,
      was incarnate of the Holy Spirit **and** the Virgin Mary
      and became truly **human**.
      For our sake he was crucified under Pontius Pilate;
   he suffered death and was buried.
      On the third day he rose again
      in accordance with the Scriptures;
      he ascended into heaven
      and is seated at the right hand of the Father.
      He will come again in glory to judge the living and the dead,
      and his kingdom will have no end.

We believe in the Holy Spirit, the Lord, the giver of life,
   who proceeds from the Father [and the Son],
   who with the Father and the Son is worshiped and glorified,
   who has spoken through the prophets.
   We believe in one holy catholic and apostolic Church.
   We acknowledge one baptism for the forgiveness of sins.
   We look for the resurrection of the dead,
      and the life of the world to come. Amen.

This is the English Language Liturgical Consultation (ELLC) translation. Formed in 1985, the Consultation is made up of representatives of the major English-speaking churches in the world. The changes from the ICET version are in bold letters and are more accurate translations of the original Greek text.

PART I

No one who has given thought to the way we talk about God can adequately grasp the terms pertaining to God. "Mother," for example, is mentioned (in the Song of Songs 3:11) instead of "father." Both terms mean the same, because there is neither male nor female in God.

St. Gregory of Nyssa
Fourth Century

The appearance of an angel to Hagar is the first incident of angelic visitation recorded in Scripture.

◆

CHAPTER ONE

WE BELIEVE IN ONE GOD

F ools say in their hearts, "There is no God." This first line of Psalm 53 reminds us that not all can say the powerful life-changing first words of the Nicene Creed, "We believe in one God."

Throughout the centuries, theologians and philosophers have grappled with how these words can be uttered with conviction. In the thirteenth century, St. Thomas Aquinas, one of the greatest classical theologians of the Christian church, used human reason to deduce that there must be a God. He postulated that if life exists, there must have been a first cause that brought life into existence. His first-cause theory sought to explain God's existence in rational terms.

Others, such as Ludwig Feuerbach, a nineteenth-century German philosopher whose writings influenced Nietzsche and Marx, used human reason to reach the opposite conclusion. He asserted that "the Christian God was nothing else than the projection of human wishes and needs. Men and women should be liberated from this illusion."[1]

Thus, human reason can devise logical constructs to prove that God both exists and does not exist. It is for this reason that we do not say as we recite the creed, "There is one God" but rather, "We believe in one God."

The Latin word for "I believe" is *credo*, from which the English word *creed* derives.[2] Thus, this statement of faith takes its name from the word for *believe*. For it is, in the final analysis, belief that is required when one speaks of God.

This first article of the Nicene Creed was originally a

profession of monotheistic faith, in opposition to the pagan belief in many gods. The creed begins with the statement that as Christian people we believe in the one true God, not in the many gods of Canaanite, Roman, or Greek culture, but in the one true God revealed through scripture.

In addition, through these first five words of the creed, Christians are linked with their Jewish and Islamic sisters and brothers throughout the world, for all three faiths profess belief in the one true God. "We believe in one God." As we say these words, if we could remember this common bond, bridges might be crossed and the bricks of the walls that can separate us might be removed one at a time.

In remembering our common bond, it is important not to forget how it was established, for to ignore the hurt that was inflicted at the inception of Islam, as recorded in Genesis, is to reinflict that pain and hurt.

The sixteenth chapter of Genesis tells us:

> Now Sarah, Abraham's wife, bore him no children. She had an Egyptian slave-girl whose name was Hagar, and Sarah said to Abraham, "You see that the Lord has prevented me from bearing children; go in to my slave-girl; it may be that I shall obtain children by her. And Abraham listened to the voice of Sarah . . . He went in to Hagar, and she conceived; and when she saw that she had conceived, she looked with contempt on her mistress . . . Then Sarah dealt harshly with her, and she ran away from her . . . Hagar bore Abraham a son; and Abraham named his son, whom Hagar bore, Ishmael . . . And Abraham said to God, "O that Ishmael might live in your sight!" God said, "No, but your wife Sarah shall bear you a son, and you shall name him Isaac. I will establish my covenant with him as an everlasting covenant for his offspring after him. As for Ishmael, I have heard you; I will bless him and make him fruitful and exceedingly numerous; he shall be the father of twelve princes, and I will make him a great nation" (Gen. 16:1, 2, 4, 6b, 15, 17-20).

As tradition has it, Ishmael's offspring became primarily the Islamic people of the world, while Isaac's offspring became the Jewish people. It is, of course, the Jewish faith that gave birth to Christianity.

Therefore, Christianity, Judaism, and Islam share a common heritage that began when both Sarah and Abraham used their Egyptian slave-girl Hagar to meet their own needs. The inequality in the relationship between these two women holds special meaning for victims of inequality today.

In her book *Just a Sister Away*, womanist biblical scholar Renita J. Weems writes: "For black women, the story of Hagar in the Old Testament book of Genesis is a haunting one. It is a story of exploitation and persecution suffered by an Egyptian slave woman at the hands of her Hebrew mistress . . . For black women, Hagar's story is peculiarly familiar. It is as if we know it by heart."[3] She goes on to state: "As black and white women in America, as Israeli and Lebanese women, as white South African and black South African women, as Asian and European women . . . working for righteousness in splendid isolation from one another is a luxury we cannot afford."[4]

As we work for righteousness in harmony with one another, it is helpful to remember the common heritage of Judaism, Christianity, and Islam that underlies the first five words of the Nicene Creed. Let us not ignore or gloss over the pain that was inflicted at the inception and throughout the history of Jewish/Islamic, Jewish/Christian, and Christian/Muslim relations. In remembering our common ancestry in all its detail, perhaps we will not repeat the mistakes of the past.

However differently these three faiths may articulate the reality of God and live out their understanding of God, the common heritage remains. This heritage finds its connecting point in Abraham, Sarah, and Hagar and in God's relationship to their offspring, yet it is often only Abraham's name that is mentioned in the liturgy of the church. It is important to remember Sarah and Hagar and their pain as women within the patriarchal tradition, a pain that was lived out in their relationship with one another. In remembering their gift to us, perhaps the ties that bind will grow ever stronger.

This tie that binds is encapsulated in the beginning of our creed, "We believe in one God." This is not to say that the writers had this in mind when the Nicene Creed was formulated - far from it. Yet, in our pluralistic world today such connections beg to be uncovered, brought into the light, and realistically examined.

Who is this God in whom we profess belief? The most frequently used Hebrew name for God, "Yahweh," tells us a great deal about who God is. "Whatever else 'Yahweh' might have connoted - it meant 'the one who is with you' (Exodus 3:12, 'I AM with you')."[5]

God is the one who is with us at our birth, throughout our life, at our death. God is the one who is with us when human constructs and situations fail us. God is the one who is with us in our suffering and pain, as well as in our relief and joy.

> But now thus says the LORD, he who created you, O Jacob, he who formed you, O Israel: Do not fear, for I have redeemed you; I have called you by name, you are mine. When you pass through the waters, I will be with you; and through the rivers, they shall not overwhelm you; when you walk through fire you shall not be burned, and the flame shall not consume you. For I am the Lord your God, the Holy One of Israel, your Savior. (Isa. 43:1-3)

Yes, "We (Christians, Jews, and Muslims) believe in one God." This one God has been with all of us throughout the troubled history of our relations. This one God must yearn for us all not to repeat the mistakes of the past.

As we recite the Nicene Creed, may we remember this common heritage and what it can mean for peace in our world today.

CHAPTER TWO

THE FATHER
ALMIGHTY

I n his catechetical lectures, delivered in the fourth century, St. Cyril of Jerusalem tells us, "This alone will be
a sufficient incentive to piety, to know that we have a
God, a God who is one, a God who is, who is eternal, who
is ever the self-same . . . who is honored under many
names."[1]

God is "honored under many names" throughout scripture and within the tradition of our faith. In Hebrew scripture, God was known by many variants of name. In
Exodus 6:2ff, we are told: "The Elohim spoke to Moses, and
he said to him, 'I am Yahweh'; and I appeared to Abraham,
to Isaac, and to Jacob as El Shaddai, but by my name
Yahweh I did not become known to them."[2] Thus, within
Hebrew scripture, God is spoken of as Elohim, Yahweh,
and El Shaddai, with Yahweh being the most frequently
used name for God.

Throughout scripture, diverse images arising out of
human experience and nature are used to describe God.[3]
These images are written as metaphors, similes, or even
descriptions of the Kingdom of God, yet all describe a God
who is indeed beyond our naming. Within scripture, God
is imaged as judge (Gen. 18:25); midwife (Ps. 22:9-10)
dew, gardener (Hos. 14:5-7); bearer and protector (Isa.
46:3-4); rock, fortress, deliverer (2 Sam. 22:2-3); daddy or
father (Mark 14:36); comforting mother (Isa. 66:13); "I
am" (Exod.3:14); good shepherd (Ps. 23:1); lion, leopard,
she-bear (Hos. 13:4-8); shepherd looking for a lost sheep

and woman searching for a lost coin (Luke 15); consuming fire (Heb. 12:29); and compassionate mother (Isa. 49:14-16).[4]

Can the totality of your experience of God be contained within one image, or are numerous images needed? The writers of scripture needed a host of images to describe the richness of their experience of God; the same is true of some of the church fathers.

For example, St. Clement of Alexandria (150-215) uses both male and female images of God. St. Clement writes: "The Word is all to the child, both father and mother, tutor and nurse."[5] Likewise, St. Ambrose (339-397), Bishop of Milan, uses both female and male imagery to describe God when he describes Jesus as being the only begotten Son from God's "paternal womb."[6] Martin Luther writes that when we suffer, God comforts us as a mother comforts a child at her breast and that through the Word and faith we receive a "profoundly paternal love and thoroughly maternal caresses."[7] In a similar vein, John Calvin writes that God is not content "with proposing the example of a father . . . but in order to express his very strong affection, he chose to liken himself to a mother."[8]

In *Legatus*, written in the thirteenth century by St. Gertrude of Helfta, God is described as a mother who uses her robe to cover a child that is too young for clothes. God is also imaged as a mother who teaches her daughter to work by guiding her hand.[9]

Thus, throughout scripture and the tradition of our church, numerous male and female images are used to refer to God. Why then was only one image for God, Father, used in the creed?

Throughout the tradition of our church, God has been referred to predominately as Father because Jesus addressed God as *abba*, which literally translated means "daddy." Through his designation of God as *abba*, Jesus expressed the extremely personal and intimate nature of his relationship with God. In *Resurrection*, Rowan Williams writes: "The Spirit is given so that we may name God as 'Father,' more exactly, as 'Abba', as *Jesus*' father

(Rom. 8:15; Gal. 4:6). 'God' appears in human history under the name of 'the one whom Jesus calls Abba.'" Even so, Williams goes on to acknowledge that "'Father' is a colossally problematic word."[10]

Whereas Jesus' naming of God as *abba* is clearly an important part of his revelation about God, it does not stand alone but in conjunction with other revelations. "Jesus' language about God is not monolithic but is diverse and colorful, as can be seen in the imaginative parables he spun out. A woman searching for her lost money, a shepherd looking for his lost sheep, a bakerwoman kneading dough . . . the birth experience that delivers persons into new life, an employer offending workers by his generosity."[11] If we take Jesus' revelations about God seriously, shouldn't we take all of his revelations into account? The use of one to the exclusion of others distorts the image of the one God who is beyond our naming, the one God clothed in divine incomprehensibility.

In *Spiritual Friend*, Tilden Edwards writes:

> The names of God in scripture reflect all kinds of images... Perhaps each of us images God in all of these ways at some time or another. At any given time, though, we likely relate more to some of these than others. Because they all express some dimension of that Ultimate Reality whose Presence we sense, it is important that a person sense their ultimate alignment. *Even though one dimension may have more value at a given point, the others correct and fill out the image. One alone can become distorting and destructive.*[12]

To understand more fully the nature of Jesus' revelation of God as Father, it is important to look at the frequency with which he refers to God in this way. In the Gospel of Mark, the oldest gospel, Jesus refers to God as Father only four times. In contrast, in the Gospel of John he refers to God as Father 101 times.[13] The Gospel of John was written some thirty years after the Gospel of Mark. This pattern led James Dunn to conclude that "here we see straightforward guidance of a burgeoning tradition, of a manner of speaking about Jesus and his relation with God which became very popular in the last decades of the first century."[14] Thus, the marked increase in Jesus' use of the term "Father" in the Gospel of John reflects theological development in the early church. It is appropriate, then, to question not only the raising up of only one of Jesus' revelations about God, but also the frequency with which Jesus made such a revelation.

God is referred to as Father in the creed for relational reasons as well. St. Cyril of Jerusalem writes: "By adding 'in One God, Father,' we combat the Jews who deny the Only-begotten Son of God . . . by the very mention of 'Father' we have already implied that He is Father of a Son . . ." [15] Thus, it was clear to early Christian theologians that "Father" is not meant to imply the *essence* of God, but rather to communicate that God is a *relational* God. Is not the designation of God as Mother equally appropriate for conveying relationship? Why, then, is only "Father" used to refer to God?

In addition to Jesus' revelation of God as *abba*, there is another reason why only the Father was mentioned as begetting the Son. In *She Who Is*, Elizabeth Johnson states: "He (Aquinas) argues that God cannot be spoken of on the analogy of mother for God is pure act, whereas in the process of begetting, the mother represents the principle that receives passively. This assumption and its attendant androcentric presuppositions permeate the classical philosophical doctrine of God as well as the specifically Christian doctrine of God's Trinity."[16] St. John of Damascus in *On the Orthodox Faith* says that "generation is 'a work of nature, producing, from the substance of the begetter, that which is begotten.' But that which is generated is produced from the semen."[17]

The belief that the semen alone begot the child, with the woman acting as mere receptacle, was widespread when the creed was formulated. This belief, of course, is no longer valid. We now know that it takes both an egg and a sperm to create new life. How can the female who contributes equally, carries, and gives birth to the child be considered merely a passive receptacle?

In light of scientific illumination, it is equally correct for us to speak of both the Father and the Mother as begetting the Son. In light of the multitude of images used by Jesus in reference to God, perhaps to balance out the use of one image alone, it is appropriate that we speak of God as both Father and Mother.

By holding up only the metaphor "Father" for God, the Nicene Creed conveys the message that God is male, which is theologically inaccurate. No credible theologian would state that God is male or female, since God is beyond sexuality or other human traits.

In keeping with this understanding, in his fourth-century commentary on the Song of Songs, St. Gregory of Nyssa writes:

> No one who has given thought to the way we talk about God can adequately grasp the terms pertaining to God. "Mother," for example, is mentioned (in the Song of Songs 3:11) instead of "father." Both terms mean the same, because there is neither male nor female in God. How, after all, could anything transitory like this be attributed to the Deity, when this is not permanent even for us human beings ... Therefore every name we invent is of the same adequacy for indicating God's ineffable nature, since neither "male" nor "female" can defile the meaning of God's pure nature.[18]

This theology is stated succinctly in the Thirty-Nine Articles of Religion, the classical theological statement of the Anglican tradition, written in the sixteenth century. Article One states: "There is but one living and true God, everlasting, *without body*, parts, or passions ... "[19]

The point has been made that God does not have a body and is therefore without gender. Yet we have only to look at Christian art throughout the centuries to see that God is portrayed almost exclusively not only as male, but as white male. Doesn't such depiction exclude not only women but all people of color from being portrayed in the image of God? Is this what God intends?

In Alice Walker's *The Color Purple*, Celie, the protagonist, writes letters to God and to her sister. She is a fourteen-year-old black girl living in the South who has been raped continuously by her stepfather. She shares the shame and degradation of her experience in letters to God. One day she says to her friend, Shug Avery, "Ain't no way to read the Bible and not think God white. When I found out I thought God was white, I lost interest." Her friend Shug responds, "My first step from the old white man was trees. Then air. Then birds. Then other people. But one day when I was sitting quiet and feeling like a motherless child, which I was, it come to me: that feeling of being part of everything, not separate at all."[20]

Thus, women of color have the dual problem not only of attempting to see beyond God as male, but of seeing beyond God as white. Images of God as different aspects of nature, which are included in scripture, are one way of moving beyond the specificity of God as any human being.

With regard to the use of exclusively male imagery for God, Elizabeth Johnson writes: "The difficulty does not lie in the fact that male metaphors are used, for men too are made in the image of God and may suitably serve as finite beginning points for reference to God. Rather, the problem consists in the fact that these male terms are used exclusively, literally, and patriarchally."[21] Is such exclusion healthy for women or men? As Sandra Schneiders points out, "It is important to recognize that the three basic life-structuring images: God, self, and world, are interrelated."[22]

It is important for all of us to be aware that religious imagery can play a complex role in a person's life. In *Women at the Well*, Kathleen Fischer writes of the "significance religious imagery has for a woman's sense of authority of the self. Images of God and self are very closely connected, and a change in one brings about a change in the other. This is borne out by testimony from contemporary women who state that a new awareness of their own authority followed upon changes in their image of God. Rather than being an external force, God became the source of a new inner power."[23]

I have found this to be true in my own life. For most of

my life, I prayed to God exclusively as Father. Without my being aware of it, when God was Father, I was little girl. At some point in my early thirties, this no longer seemed to fit, but I did not know why. My prayer life seemed blocked, God seemed distant, and I was confused. In spiritual direction and through my seminary studies, I was exposed to the wide range of imagery for God contained within scripture and tradition, and a whole new world opened up for me. I was delighted. Here was the solution to my dilemma. So I prayed to God as Mother. Nothing happened; it felt uncomfortable. So I prayed to God as Rock, the one sure foundation. This did not enhance my prayer life either. What to do?

My spiritual director suggested that I pray to "God who is beyond my naming" and perhaps God would give me an image. I have written about this part of my spiritual journey in a poem that depicts a journey taken by "this explorer and her gentle Guide." The poem is on pages 100-101.

"This explorer and her gentle Guide" have traveled many miles together since this poem was written. At different times, God has been Rock, Mother, She-bear, and yes, Father. A wide range of images for God has enriched my relationship with my creator beyond my imagining. Could the same be true for you as well? I am convinced that God is imaged in such diverse ways within scripture for a reason. How it saddens me to hear only God the Father imaged in the liturgy, creeds, and preaching of most churches. What opportunities and relationships are missed!

The need for diverse images of God can be further understood through a correct understanding of apophatic theology, which is characteristic of Eastern Christian thought dating to St. Clement of Alexandria in the second century. Apophatic theology states that God can never be conceptualized or described by human language, by asserting that God both is and is not any of the words used to image God. This *via negativa* insures against the idolatry of the affirmation of what God is, by stating that what God is, God also is not.

Contemporary theologian Sallie McFague explains

apophatic theology by stating that any image of God can only function properly and give us access to the mysterious if the "is," that is , the affirmation, and the "is not," that is, the negative qualifier, are held in tension.[24]

Similarly, St. John of Damascus writes: "Everything said of God signifies not His substance, but rather shows forth what He is not."[25] While St. Thomas Aquinas says: "For what He (God) is not is clearer than what He is."[26] This correct understanding of God-language is best understood when more than one image for God is used. When only one image is present, the "is not" qualifying tension of the image is lost and the necessary tension is absent.

For the "is" and the "is not" to be held in tension, both need to be present. For the point to be made that God is Mother, it must be stated that God is not Mother. For it to be made clear that God is Father, it must be stated that God is not Father. It is an issue of both/and rather than either/or.

Thus, it is appropriate to advocate the consistent use of both female and male imagery for God in light of numerous revelations of Jesus regarding the nature of the one God; theological assertions throughout the tradition that God is without body and therefore neither male nor female; scientific knowledge that renders invalid the concept that only the male is the begetter of a child; the need for both the "is" and "is not" qualifying tension of an image to be present, and the need for both women and men to find themselves imaged in the language used to describe God. How many substantive reasons are needed before changes in our liturgy and in our creeds can comfortably be made?

In addition to being imaged as Father in the creed, God is also described as almighty. This designation of God as almighty can be as problematic as the designation of God as Father. Many people believe somewhere in their heart of hearts that God is indeed ALMIGHTY. God can protect us from harm. God will vanquish our foes. God will somehow make it all come out the way we want.

When reality strikes, this illusion of God's almightiness, or omnipotence, can die a painful death. Questions often raised at such times are: Where is God now? Why has God deserted me? How could God let this happen? Underlying these questions is often much pain and a conception that God's almightiness means that God is an all-powerful, all-controlling puppeteer. God is reduced to superwoman or superman who can swoop down and save us as we are about to fall.

Yet God's almightiness is far from this twentieth-century view of what it means to be almighty. Contemporary theologian Letty Russell has described authority as partnership rather than domination. In applying this view of authority to an understanding of God's almightiness, we can say that God exercises God's authority in partnership with us rather than in dominion over us in a controlling, hierarchical manner. In God's Kingdom, God's power derives from God's willingness to give up power rather than to harbor it.

"So God created humankind in his image, in the image of God he created them; male and female he created them" (Gen. 1:27). In the act of creating human beings with free will, God willingly divested Godself of the ability to be almighty. God's almightiness derives from God's willingness to share that power, to give some of that power away in the loving act of creating another. How instructive such a model can be for our world today.

In addition to this model offered by Russell, Teilhard de Chardin offers another equally compelling one. In *The Divine Milieu*, he writes: "The problem of evil, that is to say the reconciling of our failures, even the purely physical ones, with creative goodness and creative power, will always remain one of the most disturbing mysteries of the universe for both our hearts and our minds."[27] He states that God's omnipotence and universal authority are manifested in the reality that "God, without sparing us the partial deaths, nor the final death, which form an essential part of our lives, transfigures them by integrating them in a better plan — *provided we trust lovingly in Him.* Not only our unavoidable ills but our faults, even our most deliberate ones, can be embraced in that transformation, provided always we repent of them. Not everything is immediately good to those who seek God; but everything is capable of becoming good: *omnia convertuntur in bonum.*"[28]

Yes, "We believe in one God, the Father, the Almighty." When I repeat these words of the Nicene Creed I am aware that God as Father was only one revelation of Jesus regarding the nature of God - a revelation that does not stand alone in Jesus' revelations or in God's self-revelation throughout scripture and the history of the church. Until the fullness of God's self-revelation is incorporated into our creedal statements, they will continue to present a partial picture of God that does not do justice to the richness and complexity of the Christian tradition.

In addition, our one God is almighty in God's willingness to give up power in the act of creating and to transfigure our misfortunes by integrating them into a far better plan.

Thanks be to God who is our comforting mother, father, rock, judge, midwife, gardener, mother bear, fortress, and deliverer.

CHAPTER THREE

MAKER OF
HEAVEN AND EARTH

O ne of my earliest childhood memories is of resting in my grandmother's plump lap while she crocheted my name in lace to go on a special pillowcase, just for me. I fell asleep to the clickety-click of her crochet needles, my head on her chest. As she hummed a tune to soothe me, her voice seemed amplified, so close was my ear to her.

What an image of God the creator my grandmother gave me - God busily creating, while continuing to nurture creation. In Psalm 139 the psalmist says to God, "For it was you who formed my inward parts; you knit me together in my mother's womb" (v. 13). In the book of Isaiah, the God who created and formed us tells each one of us, "I have called you by name, you are mine" (Isa. 43:1). God knitting us together in our mother's womb and calling us by name personifies a creator as close to us as my grandmother was to me.

Can you recall a moment of nurturing from your childhood? Was God in the midst of that experience for you?

My own childhood image of God as nurturing female creator is one that is contained in scripture in simile, metaphor, and descriptions of the activity of God. God tells the Israelites, "As a mother comforts her child, so I will comfort you" (Isa. 66:13), while the deuteronomist images God as the Rock, the creator, who gave birth to creation. "You were unmindful of the Rock that bore you; you forgot the God who gave you birth" (Deut. 32:18). God is also imaged as crying out like a woman in labor. "For a long time I have held my peace, I have kept still and restrained myself; now I will cry out like a woman in labor, I will gasp and pant" (Isa. 42:14).

God as creator, maker of heaven and earth, is also imaged with feminine language. It is not only we to whom God gives birth, but all of creation. When Job rails at God for the misfortune that has befallen him, God leads him into the mystery of creation by asking, "Who shut in the sea with doors when it burst out from the womb?" (Job 38:8) God asks further, "From whose womb did the ice come forth, and who has given birth to the hoarfrost of heaven?" (Job 38:29) The image of the sea bursting forth from God's womb, the same womb that gave birth to ice, is indeed a powerful feminine image of God as "maker of heaven and earth."

The book of Hosea contains further imagery that builds on this womb imagery for God. "Yet it was I who taught Ephraim to walk," God states. "I took them up in my arms; but they did not know that I healed them. I led them with cords of human kindness, with bands of love. I was to them like those who lift infants to their cheeks. I bent down to them and fed them" (Hos. 11:3-4).

What is the cord "of human kindness" envisioned by Hosea in this imagery of parent leading child? To answer this question, we need to look at the Hebrew words used in the phrase as well as the context in which they occur. The Hebrew words translated "cords of human kindness" are *adam chebel*, which, literally translated mean "human cords." The Hebrew word translated "bands" in the phrase "bands of love" is *aboth* which means wreathen cords.[1] "Wreathen" means formed as if by twining or interweaving.[2] Thus we have an interwoven cord of love that is a human cord. While there are different cords in the human body - the spinal cord, vocal cords, and the umbilical cord - there is only one with which someone could be led, the umbilical cord. Since this image immediately precedes the image of God as mother with a suckling child, it is highly possible that the cord alluded to by Hosea is the umbilical cord.

Thus Hosea tells us that God leads us with "cords of human kindness," the umbilical cord, that attaches us to our creator mother and nurtures us while we are still in the womb. Have you ever felt that God was leading you with "cords of human kindness"?

Building on this womb imagery for God, the maker of heaven and earth, Catholic theologian Gerald O'Collins writes:

> I want to add a comparison that can illuminate our relationship with the creator God in whom "we live and move and have our being" (Acts 17:28). Before birth we were all completely dependent on our mother for life, nourishment and growth. In her we lived and moved and had our being. She surrounded us and kept us in existence every moment. Yet it was only after our birth that our eyes were opened to see her. Can we think of our relationship to God as being now somewhat like that? Living, as it were, in the *divine womb*, we find in the creator our constant habitat and ever-present source of existence. When born into the world to come, our eyes will be opened and we will finally see that mothering God in whom we have always lived and moved and had our being.[3]

Of this passage in Acts 17 Virginia Mollenkott writes: "It is in *God* that we live, and move, and exist. Although the apostle (Paul) does not specifically name the womb, at no other time in human experience do we exist *within* another person."[4]

Thus, God is imaged in scripture as carrying the created order in the divine womb. With regard to people, the womb is not mentioned outright, but is implied. With regard to the natural order, that is the sea and the frost, God's womb is specifically mentioned.

In making these assertions, it is important to state that this should not be taken to support a position of pantheism, the belief that the created world is of God's own nature, that God is therefore a part of the natural order. These images of God as maker of heaven and earth were never meant to be taken literally. They are rather poetic images, just as are the images of God as father with hands and voice and mouth. We must remember that all of the anthropomorphic images of God are just that - images, which in and of themselves fall short of the glory that is God.

Yes, "We believe in one God . . . maker of heaven and earth." When I repeat these words of the Nicene Creed, I am reminded that God is the Rock that bore me; the God who gave me birth (Deut. 32:18). Furthermore, I feel nurtured when I remember that it is in God that "we live and move and have our being" (Acts 17:28) and that God is still leading me with "cords of human kindness" and "bands of love" (Hosea 11:4).

The clickety-click of God's crochet needles goes on in the act of creating. As each creature is named, all of us are nurtured in God's ever-present, ever-widening lap. Thanks be to God.

PART II

The Word (Christ) is everything to his little ones, both father and mother.

St. Clement of Alexandria
Second Century

As we know, our own mother bore us only into pain and dying. But our true mother Jesus, who is all love, bears us into joy and endless living.

St. Julian of Norwich
Fourteenth Century

CHAPTER FOUR

ONE LORD
JESUS CHRIST

I n the second article of the Nicene Creed, we affirm that the creator became creature.[1] How impossible this seems, yet this is the central understanding of ourselves as Christian people. It is here, in the second article, that we diverge from our Jewish and Islamic sisters and brothers. It is here that our identity as Christians, as distinct from other world religions, becomes manifest.

Karl Barth writes: "Here the hidden, the eternal and incomprehensible God has taken visible form. Here the Almighty is mighty in a quite definite, particular, earthly happening. Here the Creator Himself has become creature and therefore objective reality."[2]

In this "quite definite, particular, earthly happening" God is revealed as male. This fact leads theologian Rosemary Radford Ruether to ask, "Can a male savior save women?"[3] and leads other theologians to assert that God is revealed as male, and therefore exclusively masculine imagery and pronouns for God are appropriate. For example, Donald Bloesch insists that male language for God better expresses God's nature because "for the most part God chooses to relate himself to us as masculine"[4] (as the male Jesus). Similarly, Thomas F. Torrance writes: "In the indissoluble oneness between God and man in the person of his incarnate Son, God has once and for all incorporated *anthropic* ingredients into his self-revelation in Christ — that is, ingredients that cannot be treated as merely figurative, for they are integral to the word of God *become* flesh . . . This means that it is utterly — indeed, divinely — impossible for us to probe behind the revelation with which God has once and for all clothed himself in Jesus Christ."[5]

It is important to state that as creator became creature, the scandal of particularity was unavoidable. By the scandal of particularity, I mean all the particulars of God's "creatureliness." As Jesus Christ, God came to us as a Middle Eastern Jewish male. Yet, in discussions of the particularity of God's revelation, it is often only Jesus' maleness that is mentioned.

In my first field education parish in seminary, I vividly remember being asked, "How can you be a priest? Jesus was not female." I have since asked men of color if they have ever been asked a similar question, such as, "How can you be a priest? Jesus was not Hispanic, Asian, Black, or Korean." Not surprisingly, not one had ever encountered such a question. Thus, it is to the particularity of Jesus' maleness that I now turn.

In *Faith, Feminism, and the Christ*, Patricia Wilson-Kastner states: "To exalt the concrete details of Jesus' life in an exclusive way is to miss the whole point of the Incarnation, to misapprehend the nature of divine revelation, and in the most proper sense, to espouse heresy."[6] Why? Because throughout the tradition of our church, it is Jesus' humanity that is stressed in the incarnation, not his maleness.

Womanist theologian Jacquelyn Grant agrees. "If Jesus Christ were a Saviour of men then it is true the maleness of Christ would be paramount. But if Christ is a Saviour of all, then it is the humanity — the wholeness — of Christ which is significant."[7]

In echoing such sentiments, Wilson-Kastner and Grant take their place in a long history of Christian tradition. In his treatise *On the Incarnation*, written in the fourth century, St. Athanasius writes: "It was our sorry case that caused the Word to come down, our transgression that called out His love for us, so that He made haste to help us and to appear among us. It is we who were the cause of

His taking human form, and for our salvation that in His great love He was both born and manifested in a human body."[8]

St. Athanasius is asserting here that the significance of the incarnation is that God assumed *human* form, not that God assumed a *male* form. Athanasius goes on to state that "what has not been assumed has not been redeemed."[9] Since Jesus is the redeemer of all humankind, God assumed human form, which of necessity had to be either male or female. Since Jesus came to save all of humankind and in Christ "there is no longer male and female" (Gal. 3:28), it is not gender that is of significance, but Jesus' humanity.

St. Paul also stresses Jesus' humanity rather than his maleness, in the great Christological hymn in Philippians 2:5-11:

Let the same mind be in you that was in Christ Jesus,
who, though he was in the form of God,
did not regard equality with God as something to be
exploited,
but emptied himself
taking the form of a slave
being born in human likeness.
And being found in human form
he humbled himself
and became obedient to the point of death —
even death on a cross. (Phil. 2:5 - 8)

In this passage, St. Paul could have used the Greek word *aner*, meaning "male" but instead he uses the word *anthropos*, which means "human."

Similarly, a homily written by St. Basil of Caesarea in 379 states: "God on earth, God among us! No longer the God who gives his law amid flashes of lightening . . . but the God who speaks gently and with kindness in a human body to his kindred."[10]

In 389, St. Gregory of Nazianzus wrote: "Conceived of the Virgin who had been purified by the Spirit in her body and soul, it is truly God who assumes humanity ..."[11]

Thus, it is clear throughout the tradition of our church

and in scripture itself that it is God's assumption of human form that is of significance in the incarnation, not God's assumption of a male form.

Perhaps it is to make just such a distinction that Jesus refers to himself as a mother hen in both Matthew and Luke. In imaging himself as a female bird, Jesus moves beyond the constraints of the particularity of the incarnation. "Jerusalem, Jerusalem, the city that kills the prophets and stones those who are sent to it! How often have I desired to gather your children together as a hen gathers her brood under her wings, and you were not willing!" (Matt. 23:37; Luke 13:34).

Jesus knew, when he compared himself to a mother hen, that he was using a well-known image for God from the Hebrew scriptures. "Certainly the author of 2 Esdras, an apocryphal book dating from the first century C.E., understood Jesus' hen image as tapping into a Hebrew understanding of God as both father and mother and internal authentic Self."[12] 2 Esdras 1:28 - 30 states: "Thus says the Lord Almighty; Have I not entreated you as a father entreats his sons or a mother her daughters or a nurse her children, so that you should be my people and I should be your God, and that you should be my children and I should be your father? I gathered you as a hen gathers her chicks under her wings."

Jesus' imaging of himself as mother hen was compelling enough to be quoted by both St. Augustine and St. Anselm of Canterbury, two men of immense theological importance in Western Christianity. In the fourth century, St. Augustine wrote: "Let us put our egg under the wings of that Hen of the Gospel, which crieth out to that false and abandoned city, 'O Jerusalem, Jerusalem, how often would I have gathered thy children together, even as a hen her chickens, and thou wouldest not!'"[13] Similarly, St. Anselm, who became Archbishop of Canterbury in 1093, wrote: "But you, Jesus, good lord, are you not also a mother? Are you not that mother who, like a hen, collects her chickens under her wings? Truly, master, you are a mother."[14]

If Jesus, St. Augustine, and St. Anselm of Canterbury

can all image Jesus as mother hen, why is similar imaging so difficult for us today? The Supplemental Liturgical Texts of 1989 was a trial liturgy in the Episcopal Church using inclusive imagery for God and Jesus, taken from scripture. The service of Holy Communion stated: "Living among us, Jesus loved us. He yearned to draw all the world to himself, as a hen gathers her young under her wings, yet we would not . . ."[15] Labeled as "too controversial" this section was changed in subsequent trial liturgies to, "He yearned to draw all the world to himself yet we were heedless of his call to walk in love."[16]

Perhaps this imagery was labeled controversial because most people focus on the "quite definite, particular, earthly happening,"[17] as Barth mentions. The earthly happening was indeed male, yet, as male, Jesus imaged himself as mother hen.

Furthermore, while the incarnate Christ was male, it can be argued that the pre-incarnate Word is without body and therefore, like the first person of the Trinity, is neither male nor female. In writing of the pre-existent Christ, the Word, in the fourth century, St. Athanasius states: "He has not assumed a body as proper to His own nature, far from it, for *as the Word He is without body.*"[18]

Contemporary Lutheran theologian Robert W. Bertram agrees: "By now it should no longer be necessary (though alas it is) to demonstrate that Jesus' addressing God as '*Abba*' and 'Father' hardly implies that God is male, any more than the pre-incarnate 'Son' is."[19]

Although some theologians such as St. Thomas Aquinas and John Calvin view Christ's ascension as bodily, others view it as the ascension of a spiritual body in keeping with Pauline theology. In his first letter to the Corinthians, St. Paul asserts: "So it is with the resurrection of the dead. What is sown is perishable, what is raised is imperishable. It is sown in dishonor, it is raised in glory. It is sown in weakness, it is raised in power. It is sown a physical body, it is raised a spiritual body" (1 Cor. 15:42-44).

In line with this Pauline understanding, Anglican theologian Sarah Coakley stated in a speech given at the

Lambeth Conference in 1988: "Of course Jesus of Nazareth was indisputably a man, but surely we cannot say that the risen Christ, the second person of the Trinity, is physically male, any more than we really want to say ... that the Father is a man."[20]

In making such an assertion, it must be noted that whereas the incarnation had a beginning, it has not ended. In *Loving the Questions*, Marianne H. Micks writes: "It was Jesus of Nazareth, the incarnate Logos, who was resurrected and who ascended. Humanity is bonded to divinity for all time."[21]

Coakley's assertion is not meant to suggest that the incarnation is negated when Christ ascends. It means, rather, that the risen and ascended Christ is beyond the boundaries of sexual distinction. It is humanity that is bonded to divinity for all time, not mere maleness. Coakley's statement facilitates this correct theological understanding of the incarnation.

In addition, it is important to stress that throughout the Christian tradition, even the incarnate Christ, Jesus of Nazareth, was consistently imaged as both male and female. It is for this reason that Anglican theologian Mary Tanner stated at the Lambeth Conference of 1988 that the church needs to "recapture certain neglected strands of the tradition, especially from the mystics of the church, that help to point our way into the future."[22]

Recapturing and recovering lost tradition is what I am suggesting here, not inventing something out of whole cloth to answer only a twentieth-century concern. As committed Christians isn't it appropriate that we teach all of the tradition of our church rather than just part of it?

One of the earliest images of Jesus as both male and female was written in the second century by St. Clement of Alexandria: "The Word (Christ) is everything to His little ones, both father and mother."[23] Similarly, in his *Baptismal Instructions*, St. John Chrysostom writes: "Just as a woman nurtures her offspring with her own blood and milk, so also Christ continuously nurtures with his own blood those whom He has begotten."[24]

St. Augustine speaks of Christ as a nursing mother: "He who has promised us heavenly food has nourished us on milk, having recourse to a mother's tenderness. For just as a mother, suckling her infant, transfers from her flesh the very same food which otherwise would be unsuited to a babe . . . so our Lord, in order to convert His wisdom into milk for our benefit came to us clothed in flesh."[25] In his *Confessions* he wrote, "For 'the Word was made flesh,' that Thy wisdom, whereby Thou createdst all things, might provide milk for our infant state."[26]

In the twelfth century, St. Bernard of Clairvaux also refers to Jesus as mother: "Do not let the roughness of our life frighten your tender years. If you feel the stings of temptation . . . suck not so much the wounds as the breasts of the Crucified. He will be your mother, and you will be his son."[27] Similarly, in the fourteenth century, St. Catherine of Siena wrote to Pope Urban VI, urging him to "amend in truth those who are feeding at the breast of your sweet Spouse."[28]

In addition, Julian of Norwich, a fourteenth-century English anchoress, observes: "As we know, our own mother bore us only into pain and dying. But our true mother Jesus, who is all love, bears us into joy and endless living."[29] In her book of revelations, *Showings*, she goes on to state: "(When we are afraid, Christ) wants us to act as a meek child, saying: My kind Mother, my gracious Mother, my beloved Mother, have mercy on me . . . The sweet and gracious hands of our Mother are ready and diligent about us; for (Christ) in all this work exercises the true office of a kind nurse, who has nothing else to do but attend to the safety of her child."[30]

For an excellent discussion of Jesus as mother, see Caroline Walker Bynum's *Jesus as Mother: Studies in the Spirituality of the High Middle Ages.*

Contemporary theologian William Eichelberger sees Jesus not only as female, but as Black female: "It is my feeling that God is now manifesting Himself, and has been for over 450 years, in the form of the Black American Woman as mother, as wife, as nourisher, sustainer and preserver of life, the Suffering Servant who is despised and rejected by men (sic), a personality of sorrow who is acquainted with grief."[31] In my own life I have been blessed by knowing two such women, who through their love and caring taught me much about the love of God, Anner Weakley and Annie Ruth Livingston. Knowing them makes Eichelberger's assertion seem quite plausible to me.

When I first began reading of Christ as female, I was definitely confused. How could anyone think of Jesus Christ, so obviously a male, as female? I was, of course, focusing on the "particular earthly happening" of the second person of the Trinity as discussed by Barth. The concept of Christ as female had never occurred to me. And why would it? Such teaching is hardly part of most Sunday School curricula. Even so, saints and theologians throughout the history of Christianity have referred to Jesus as mother.

In the twelfth century, St. Hildegard of Bingen had a vision of Christ as female:

> During the celebration on the eve of our Lord's Nativity, around the hour of the divine sacrifice, I entered a trance and saw something like a sun of marvelous brightness in the heaven, and in the middle of the sun the likeness of a virgin whose appearance was exceedingly beautiful in form and desirable to see. She was seated on a throne. Her hair was loosened over her shoulders, and on her head was a crown of the most splendid gold. In her right hand was a golden chalice. She was emerging from the sun which surrounded her on all sides. From the virgin herself emanated a splendor of great brilliance, which seemed at first to fill the place of our dwelling. Then gradually expanding after some period of time, it seemed to fill the whole earth.
>
> Now next to that same sun there appeared a great cloud, extremely dark and horrible to see. When I gazed at the cloud, it rushed abruptly against the sun, darkened it, and cut off its splendor from the earth for some time. I saw this happen very often, moreover, so that the world was by turns darkened by the cloud and again illuminated by the sun. Whenever it happened that the cloud approached the sun and obstructed its light from the earth, the virgin who was enthroned within the sun seemed to be weeping copiously, as if grieving greatly because of the darkening of the

world. I beheld this vision throughout that day without interruption, and all the following night, for I remained ever wakeful in prayer.

On the holy day of Christmas, now, when the solemnities of the masses were being celebrated, I asked the holy angel of God who appeared to me what sort of vision that was and what significance it had. He replied to me concerning that virgin, for I especially desired to know who she was, and he said: "That virgin who you see is the sacred humanity of the Lord Jesus."[32]

Just as female images for God can be healing for both women and men, so too can feminine images of Jesus that have been used throughout the tradition of our church. Kathleen Fischer observes: "Theological assertions that the risen Christ transcends the concrete particulars of history do not have the power that a single image has to bring about this emotional healing and focus for worship. Women's imaginations need the deep emotional healing and affirmation that come from seeing the image and likeness of Christ conveyed more fully in relation to them . . . To say that Christ cannot be imaged as a woman is to imply that women cannot, in fact, image Christ."[33] What might it do to your self-image never to see yourself in the likeness of Christ? How might the world be different if both women and men could be seen in Christ's image?

Yes, "We believe in one Lord Jesus Christ." When I repeat these words of the Nicene Creed, I mean: "I believe in one Lord Jesus Christ, who is imaged as both male and female, by Jesus himself and throughout the tradition of our church."

When will this tradition be recovered in the liturgy and creeds of our church? When will there be another ecumenical council to consider this question?

*"I am both God and flesh.
I am the image of father
and of mother."*
(Translation of Latin in the mosaic)

Virgin and Child with Apostles, 12th century. Apse mosaic.
Cattedrale di S. Maria Assunta, Torcello, Italy.
Photo credit: Alinari/Art Resource, NY.

CHAPTER FIVE

THE ONLY
SON OF GOD

N eedless to say, the issue of masculine and feminine imagery for Jesus was hardly a concern when the creeds were being formulated. The christological controversy of the fourth century involved the question of Jesus' humanity and divinity.

This question arose at a particular time in the history of the Christian church. It is important to place the controversy within its proper historical context. The first Council of Nicea met in 325, thirteen years after a major turning point in Christian history. In 312, Constantine entered Rome as victor. When he became emperor he granted all Christians full freedom of worship. Before his victory, Christians who publicly confessed their faith were persecuted. Once the persecutions ended and pressure from the central government was removed, intra-Christian issues began to emerge.[1] One such issue was related to the identity of Jesus as both God and human.

Arius was an Alexandrian presbyter who believed that the Logos, or second person of the Trinity, could not be God in the proper sense but instead performed a mediatorial role in the relation of God to the world. He believed that the Logos belonged to the created order and was "a quite superior creature, ranking above all others."[2] Nevertheless, the Logos was not God.

St. Athanasius, on the other hand, believed that "redemption can occur only through God's active presence with people . . . His understanding of redemption made no sense if the Logos was a being 'between' the divine and the human. It made sense only if the Logos was God's way of being personally present and active in the world."[3]

Arius' position was repudiated in the creed formulated at the Council of Nicaea in 325. The creed declares that "the Logos is not a creature but is eternally born out of God himself and is therefore divine in the same sense as the Father."[4] Hence the words in the Nicene Creed, "the only Son of God, eternally begotten of the Father, God from God, Light from Light, true God from true God, begotten, not made, of one Being with the Father."

In *The Making of the Creeds*, Frances Young states: "The one Lord was 'of the same substance' as the Father, one God identical in substance, action and will . . . It really was God, God's self, who was born in the Lord Jesus Christ."[5]

When I say that Jesus is of one being with the Father, I am asserting that he is of one being with the first person of the Trinity, who is described in scripture with numerous images, one of which is Father. In the tradition of apophatic theology, discussed earlier, just as the first person of the Trinity is Father, the first person is not Father. Just as the first person is Mother, the first person is not Mother. Just as the first person is Rock, the first person is not Rock.

In keeping with this tradition, the Eleventh Council of Toledo in Spain left us a long creed that presented the Son as being generated "from the womb of the Father."[6]

The juxtaposition of such images breaks down irreparably any use of one image as an absolute. Whatever one might say after mentioning "the womb of the Father," the masculine and feminine are never the same. Throughout the history of our church, such images have been placed side by side with an awareness that it expresses that God is this and also that, that none of the images can be taken literally.

In addition, in reciting the second article of the creed, I am stating that Christ is of one Being with God who is beyond gender. Classical theology has always held that God is beyond gender, even while imaging God with primarily male imagery. If the creed states that the second person of the Trinity is "of one Being" with the first, does it not follow that Christ, too, must of necessity be eternally and essentially beyond gender distinctions? How can a gender-bound being be of the same substance, or *homoousios*, with a being beyond gender restrictions? Yes, the incarnate Christ was male, which belongs to Christ's person, or *hypostasis*. However, his substance, or *ousia*, belongs to the universal and is beyond gender designation.

In addition to referring to Jesus as *homoousios* with God, sources from the early church refer to Jesus as the "child" of God, rather than exclusively as the "Son" of God. The first written record of a eucharistic service is contained in the *Apostolic Tradition of Hippolytus*, written in the early third century. In this service, Jesus is referred to twice as "child" rather than "son": "We render thanks to you, O God, through your beloved child Jesus Christ, whom in the last times you sent to us a saviour and redeemer and angel of your will."[7] Further, "that we may praise and glorify you through your child Jesus Christ."[8]

This service refers to Jesus as both the child and the son of God. This reference to Jesus as the "child of God" enables both women and men to feel included in such a description. It also does justice to Jesus' use of maternal images of himself, as well as the witness of numerous church fathers and theologians of both male and female images of Christ.

Yes, "We believe in one Lord, Jesus Christ . . . of one Being with the Father." In making this assertion, I am conscious that if the Father is beyond gender distinction and Jesus is of "one being with the Father", then Jesus too, must essentially and eternally be beyond gender designation. This fact bears significant relevance to a correct theological understanding of who Jesus is and will be discussed in more depth in chapter IX on the Trinity.

May the light shine on this and other truths regarding the nature of our Lord and Savior Jesus Christ, the only child of God.

CHAPTER SIX

INCARNATE FROM THE VIRGIN MARY

One fall several years ago, I accompanied a youth group on a diocesan retreat to Medford Lakes, New Jersey. On the retreat I served as a counselor to seventy-five twelve and thirteen-year-olds.

The first night we were there, the diocesan youth director, Toni Daniels, was giving us instructions in the large dining hall. Suddenly she was interrupted by a young woman tugging at her sleeve, whispering something urgent to her. To my surprise, Toni ignored her. So the young woman continued to interrupt, then pleaded with her, saying, "Toni, you've got to help me! I've got to talk to you now!" Giving her the cold shoulder, Toni answered, "I don't have time right now. Can't you see I'm busy?" The entire exchange made many of us uneasy, for we were beginning to feel concern for this young woman. After her pleas went unanswered, in desperation she finally blurted out, "Toni, I'm pregnant!" Then she rushed out of the dining hall.

Just as we were all beginning to digest what had happened, a man dressed in animal skins ran into the hall shouting, "Prepare ye the way of the Lord!" He urged us to follow him, and follow him we did down to the edge of Medford Lake.

By this point, I had reached the conclusion that these actors were portraying the Virgin Mary and John the Baptist, but many of the middle school students had not. As we stood around the lake while the Baptist baptized, I was intrigued by the conversation taking place around me. "Do you think this is for real or not? I mean, she looked pretty scared to me! Did you see her face and the look in her eyes?" "You know, she mainly looked confused to me, startled and surprised. I think we should try to help her. She's got to be in big trouble with her parents." The conversation and concern for this young woman continued.

As we walked back up the hill together, I could not help pondering the difference between the Mary that had just been presented to us and the Mary I had come to know, or not know, through scripture and centuries of Christian art.

The Mary I had come to know was Mother Mary, meek and mild; Mother Mary depicted with an angelic smile on her face as the angel Gabriel announces what must have been shocking news to her; Mother Mary who had no real say in what was about to happen to her.

The difference between the Mary I had come to know and the Mary at Medford Lakes was that the young woman who rushed in, tugging at Toni's sleeve and pleading with her, was real. She had emotions, concerns, even fright over her situation. She was a far cry from the placidly smiling European-looking Mary, with the dove flying over her head, who has been rendered immortal by the stroke of an artist's brush.[1]

Who is the real Mary? Does scripture offer us any clues?

As recorded in Luke's annunciation story, Mary's initial response to the angel is one of fear, prompting Gabriel to reassure her, "Do not be afraid, Mary" (Luke 1:30). She was fearful of God's powerful intervention in her life. Who among us is not as fearful as Mary was, when God demands our attention in a way that we can no longer ignore?

In addition, the evangelist writes that following the annunciation, Mary left with haste to the hill country to visit Elizabeth, who was pregnant with John the Baptist. Not only did Mary leave with haste, but she stayed with Elizabeth for three months. Perhaps she too, needed to rush to the side of a trusted friend and share her news.

In *Just A Sister Away*, Renita J. Weems wonders about

46

this special time Mary and Elizabeth spent together:

> What the two women talked about, we can only imagine. No doubt they shared stories about the changes their bodies were undergoing. They probably touched one another's protruding bellies and massaged one another's swollen feet. They certainly laughed . . . and cried . . . and reminisced . . . and dreamed. And they most likely imagined the kinds of men their sons would grow up to be.
>
> The two women shared with one another things they could never share with the men in their lives. They held on to one another for dear life. They were women trying to grapple with the hand of God in their lives, sharing with each other the blessednesses and the burdensomeness of being blessed.[2]

Mary's need for companionship at such a time is a feeling most of us can relate to, although it has always been difficult for me to make any real connection with Mary as a woman, for connecting with her as a woman is difficult. The traditional picture of Mary is one in which her virginity and her motherhood are accentuated at one and the same time. Who among us can emulate that? Although the church has concentrated on these aspects of the Marian tradition, are they the most important of what Luke has to tell us about Mary in his annunciation scene?

Pope Paul VI wrote: "She (Mary) is held up as an example to the faithful for the way in which in her own particular life she fully and responsibly accepted the will of God, because she heard the word of God and acted on it . . . She is worthy of imitation because she was the first and most perfect disciple."[3]

How many of us have ever been taught that Mary was the "first and most perfect disciple?" Yet in Luke's gospel, Mary becomes a disciple because she hears the word of God, believes it, and acts on that belief. Mary becomes the first disciple, indeed the first Christian, by hearing the good news of Jesus' identity as Messiah and God's son, and by accepting it.

The importance of Mary's faith to each one of us cannot be stressed enough, for Mary's faith makes possible God's entrance into history.[4] If Mary had not responded affirmatively to the angel Gabriel, how might your life be different?

It is possible that Mary could have said "no." Instead, she made her affirmative "yes" to God's plan for the salvation of all when she said, "Behold I am the handmaid of the Lord; let it be to me according to your word" (Luke 1:38, RSV).

The word *handmaid* sounds poetic to us today, but is actually the feminine form of the word for "slave." Mary is a disciple because she hears the word of God, accepts it, and acts on it by responding, "Yes, I am the slave of the Lord; let it be with me according to your word." The birth of the Messiah, the embodiment of the future redemption of the world, is dependent on Mary's affirmative to God's plan.

Through Mary's affirmative response, not only did she become the first disciple, but, at the Council of Ephesus in 431, she was accorded the designation *Theotokos*, or God-bearer. At this council, Nestorius argued that Mary was *Christokos*, bearer of Christ, but not *Theotokos*. "The creature," he asserted of Mary, "did not bear the uncreated Creator."[5] But Cyril of Alexandria argued that Mary was indeed the bearer of God. His argument ultimately prevailed.

Anglican historian J. Robert Wright states:

> The controversy around Nestorius and Ephesus was primarily a Christological controversy, not a Mariological one, although it did have Mariological implications. For instance, whereas prior to Ephesus depictions of Mary in Christian art usually show her as one figure in a scene (e.g. Nativity, Adoration of Magi, etc.), after Ephesus she is more and more portrayed on her own as the Holy Theotokos.[6]

One such portrayal of significance is the Icon of Our Lady of the Sign, in which Mary is in the "orans" position, with hands outstretched in prayer, and Christ is depicted in her womb. In this icon, Mary is generating Christ.

In the Roman Catholic and Orthodox faiths, one argument against the ordination of women to the priesthood is that a woman priest cannot generate Christ at the Eucharist. Only a male priest can "impregnate" the host. Yet here, in traditional iconography following the Council of Ephesus, Mary is indeed generating Christ.

Thus, within the tradition, Mary is not only the first and most perfect disciple, she also stands alone as the *Theotokos* or bearer of God. In fact, "the Episcopal Church addresses her as 'Thou *bearer* of the eternal Word' in Hymn 618."[7]

Interestingly, a fifteenth-century Swabian painting of the Eucharist, *Retable of the Mystical Mill,* goes one step further. Here, Mary, with the assistance of the four evangelists is depicted as the miller, or celebrant, generating Christ at the eucharistic table, while the assembled prelates kneel humbly below to receive the food of God. This illustration is reproduced on page 52.

In addition, there is more here for us who seek to know Mary. In her article "The Story of Mary: Luke's Version," Deborah F. Middleton asserts that only one other place in scripture refers to a child, or children, without a natural father. Adam and Eve come into existence only through the creative power of God. According to Luke, the Holy Spirit is to come upon Mary just as it had come upon the watery chaos at the beginning of time, when the world was created. The presence of the Spirit marks the presence of God and in Luke, as in the first chapter of Genesis, it marks the moment of creation. In this new creation Mary is to be God's partner, and together they will create the New Adam, as St. Paul often calls Jesus. In her willingness to take part in God's plan, Mary becomes co-creator with God.[8] This understanding of Mary is reflected in the Roman Catholic Church's traditional portrayal of her as Co-redemptrix.

Thus, what we have is Mary, the first disciple, who heard the word of God and believed it; Mary, who acted on that belief by willingly playing an active role in God's plan for salvation; Mary, God's co-creator of the new Adam and the new Israel, making possible a new life for all through

Jesus Christ.

What a model Mary can be for women and men in our world today. For, like Mary, our call is to hear the word of God, to believe it, and then to act upon that belief. In those special moments in our lives when we hear God's call to us, may we have the courage as Mary did to answer, "Let it be with me according to your word" (Luke 1:38).

The active rather than the passive role of Mary in the annunciation is, in fact, reflected in the original Greek text of the Nicene Creed. The English Language Liturgical Consultation (ELLC), a body made of representatives of the main liturgical churches (Roman Catholic, Anglican, and Lutheran), was established in 1985 to deal with interdenominational English-language liturgical matters. This body has asserted that the Nicene Creed, correctly translated from the Greek, should be changed from "he became incarnate from the Virgin Mary and was made man" to "was incarnate of the Holy Spirit *and* the Virgin Mary and became truly *human*."[9]

With regard to the ICET translation of the creed which the ELLC has corrected, J. Robert Wright notes:

> Literally, the original Greek text of Chalcedon 451 reads "Of the Holy Spirit *and (kai)* the Virgin Mary," the conjunction *and* emphasizing the cooperative relationship of Mary and the Spirit. By a slip of spelling in the Latin version, the Latin *et* (for the Greek *kai*), meaning "and," slid into *ex*, meaning "from," which produced the western mistranslation "by the Holy Spirit *from* the Virgin Mary," perpetuated here, which thus presented Mary as a mere passive vessel in the incarnation rather than actively consenting, cooperating, and working together with God. This is the least accurate point in the ICET translation.[10]

In addition, it is very important to a correct christological understanding of the creed to note that the change from "became truly man" to "became truly human" is also a more accurate translation of the original Greek text. The Greek word that has been translated "man" in the ICET translation is *anthropos*, which means "human." There is another Greek word *aner*, which means "male" that could have been used, but was not.

Why? Because as articulated in Chapter IV, it is Jesus' humanity that is operative in the incarnation, not his maleness. St. Paul, St. Athanasius, St. Basil, St. Gregory of Nazianzus, and others all stress Jesus' humanity in the incarnation, rather than his maleness. In our own day, Anglican historian Richard A. Norris, Jr. does the same in "The Beginnings of Christian Priesthood," in which he writes of "the joining of God and humanity in Christ."[11]

Yes, "by the power of the Holy Spirit he became incarnate from the Virgin Mary, and was made man." When I recite these words, I am conscious of the fact that the original Greek text states, "Of the Holy Spirit *and* the Virgin Mary", emphasizing the cooperative relationship between Mary, the first and most perfect disciple, and the Holy Spirit.

Furthermore, I am aware that "man" is an inaccurate translation of the original Greek text that reflects a theological inaccuracy each time it is repeated, for it is Jesus' humanity that is of significance in the incarnation, not his maleness, as demonstrated in scripture and by theologians throughout the history of the Christian church.

When will these corrections be incorporated in the translation of the Nicene Creed that is recited throughout Christendom?

This Swabian painting of the Eucharist depicts Mary as miller, or celebrant, assisted by the four evangelists. The assembled prelates kneel humbly below to receive the food of God.

Retable of the Mystical Mill: Mary surrounded by the Evangelsts serving the Eucharist, circa 1440. Artist Unknown.
Ulmer Museum, Schmatz, Germany.
Photo credit: Foto Marburg/Art Resource, NY.

CHAPTER SEVEN

HE WAS
CRUCIFIED

D uring a recent Good Friday service, a young black
woman sang with all her heart and soul, "Were You
There When They Crucified My Lord?" The pathos
of the crucifixion was communicated through her words,
the anguish through her posture and body movement. It
seemed as if she were standing at the foot of the cross, witnessing the crucifixion of her Lord and Savior.

As her song filled every crevice and space of the church,
my mind was filled with images of the women who did
stand at the foot of the cross, for it was the women who
stayed, while every apostle except John fled. John's gospel
states: "Meanwhile, standing near the cross of Jesus were
his mother, and his mother's sister, Mary the wife of Clopas,
and Mary Magdalene. When Jesus saw his mother and the
disciple whom he loved standing beside her, he said to his
mother, 'Woman, here is your son'" (John 19:25-26).

Mark's gospel tells us that "Mary Magdalene, and Mary
the mother of James the younger and of Joses, and
Salome" (Mark 15:40) stayed with Jesus. Matthew's gospel
relates that "Mary Magdalene, and Mary the mother of
James and Joseph, and the mother of the sons of Zebedee"
(Matt. 27:56) were present. None of the synoptic gospels
mentions John as being part of the group.

Why did the women stay while most of the male apostles fled? In her book *Are Women Human?*, Dorothy L.
Sayers suggests one possibility:

Perhaps it is no wonder that the women were first at the

Cradle and last at the Cross. They had never known a man like this Man — there never has been such another. A prophet and teacher who never nagged at them, never flattered or coaxed or patronized; who never made arch jokes about them, never treated them either as "The women, God help us!" or "The ladies, God bless them!"; who rebuked without querulousness and praised without condescension; who took their questions and arguments seriously; who never mapped out their sphere for them, never urged them to be feminine or jeered at them for being female; who had no axe to grind and no uneasy male dignity to defend; who took them as he found them and was completely unself-conscious. There is no act, no sermon, no parable in the whole Gospel that borrows its pungency from female perversity; nobody could possibly guess from the words and deeds of Jesus that there was anything "funny" about woman's nature.[1]

Furthermore, the women may have been last at the cross because they could identify with Jesus' suffering at the hands of an unjust system, a system in which they, as women, were regarded as mere property of men. Such identification is suggested by both contemporary Black women and women in developing nations.

Throughout history, women of color have identified Jesus' suffering with their own. In "Womanist Theology: Black Women's Experience," Jacquelyn Grant writes: "For Christian Black women in the past, Jesus was their central frame of reference. They identified with Jesus because they believed that Jesus identified with them. *As Jesus was persecuted and made to suffer undeservedly so were they.*"[2] Jesus is viewed as the "divine co-sufferer, who empowers them in situations of oppression."[3]

Similarly, at the "Women and the Christ-event Workshop" at the Manila Consultation in the Philippines, November 1985, Lydia Lascano, a delegate from the Philippines stated that Jesus' passion was an act of solidarity with his people. "He assured them of the promised reign of God while he responded to their concrete needs and their questions on life's contradictions. Because of this he endured suffering at the hands of his captors. The suffering was a further act of identification with his people who saw no clear end to their misery at the hands of the system."[4]

If Black women and women in developing nations can see Jesus' suffering as in solidarity with their own, perhaps so too did the women who stood at the foot of the cross so long ago. Perhaps Jesus' writhing in pain and exhaustion mirrored their own pain and exhaustion. His suffering was theirs and theirs was his. Perhaps this is the bond that held them transfixed on that hill on Calvary so long ago.

Through the crucifixion, God experiences something not unlike the desperate pain of dying in childbirth. The agony of Christ on the cross is the agony of the birth pangs of a new creation. The new creation first becomes a reality when the empty tomb, womb-like, is discovered. As after the birth, the body is expelled, no longer held in the womb-tomb.

Christ giving birth to the church on the cross is vividly depicted in a thirteenth-century French Moralized Bible in Oxford, England. The church, depicted as a baby, is being born out of Christ's side. This illumination can be found on page 60.

While it may not be difficult to identify ourselves with the suffering Christ, how many of us identify ourselves with the angry mob that called for his crucifixion? How much easier it is to see ourselves as victim rather than victimizer. Yet as a well-educated, economically comfortable white woman I know that I benefit from a system that discriminates and works against the poor and the marginalized. If in the cross of Christ I can only see my own suffering, or the suffering of those close to me, I have failed to grasp the depth of meaning the cross contains.

Several years ago on Palm Sunday I preached a sermon on the passion narrative in Matthew's gospel. A dramatic reading of the narrative had just taken place in which the congregation is the angry mob that yells, "Let him be crucified. Let him be crucified." I would like to share that sermon with you here because it highlights the significance of the crufixion experience for women who struggle daily to survive in our inner cities. The message it conveys further illuminates the meaning of the crucifixion for me and it might shed new light on the crucifixion for you as well.

Matthew 26:36 - 27:66

"Let him be crucified. Let him be crucified."

All of us who attend the Palm Sunday liturgy, find ourselves participating in the gospel narrative. Regardless of how we may feel, we suddenly find ourselves shouting, "Let him be crucified." In that moment, we are transformed from a Sunday morning group of worshippers into the very first-century people who crucified Jesus. This is not a neutral crowd of which we're suddenly a part. Neither is it an innocent crowd. For there are no uninvolved bystanders here, but rather we are a crowd of people with blood on our hands.

Every Palm Sunday when I shout, "Let him be crucified," it is a heart-rending experience for me. I don't want to become part of the angry mob. I want to step back from it and say, "Stop! Don't you know who it is that you are crucifying?" But having the text in my hands I know I can't do that. Even so, part of me thinks, "Isn't there anybody who cares enough to take that risk?"

One of the distinctive features of Matthew's passion narrative is that someone does take that risk. For while Pilate is sitting on the judgment seat, his wife sends word to him: "Have nothing to do with that innocent man, for today I have suffered a great deal because of a dream about him" (Matt. 27:19).

So Pilate's wife has a dream, a revelation regarding Jesus' righteousness, prompting her to send word to her husband attesting to the innocence of Jesus. As a result of her disturbing revelation, she tells us that this whole proceeding is evil.

Yet her attempt fails. For even though Pilate then questions the crowd's reasons for wanting Jesus crucified, the outcome is not changed. So her action has no more effect on this narrative than would our action today if we had boldly stepped back from this crowd and shouted, "Stop!" No, we can't put this film in reverse. Nor can we stop it or erase it. We are part of the crowd with blood on its hands that calls for the crucifixion of Jesus of Nazareth.

As part of this crowd, we become part of the system that

crucifies Jesus — a system in which Jesus is rejected by the leaders of Israel, betrayed by Judas, deserted by his apostles, condemned by his council, denied by Peter, and implicated by the crowd of which we are a part. He is then whipped, mocked, spat upon, hit on the head, and finally nailed to the cross.

But why are we on Palm Sunday made to be part of the mob that crucifies Jesus? I don't like being part of this scene. Do you? We would *never* crucify Jesus. *Never*. Or would we? Or do we? Could it be that *we* crucify Jesus?

To begin to answer this question, we need to shift settings from first-century Jerusalem to a twentieth-century urban ministry where I was a high school equivalency instructor at a Catholic settlement house. One of my students there was a twenty-eight-year-old mother of four.

Before attending our class, she had worked in a factory putting price tags on newly-made clothes. However, she soon found not only that the day care she could afford was substandard, but also that her pay check could not even cover her day-care costs. At the time she came to our class, her husband had found work, which enabled her to study for her high school equivalency diploma.

As the year progressed, it became apparent that she was trapped in an abusive relationship with her spouse. She wanted to leave, but she was afraid. What would she do? Where would she go? One morning she came in brighter and more cheerful than I had seen her in months. "I've left!" she said. "I'm through with being treated like that. I've taken my children and I've found another place." Unknown to me at that time, the only place she had been able to afford had thirteen building code violations. The Division of Youth and Family Services of New Jersey found out, took her children away from her, and placed them in separate foster homes.

I will never forget the morning she told me what had happened. We were working on reading comprehension that day when she asked me a question and suddenly burst into tears. I then took her into a room behind our class that functioned as a used clothing store for the community.

In the midst of the smell of musty clothes and worn shoes piled high, she told me that she ached to see her children. I was shocked and angered that this could happen when she had finally had the courage to leave an intolerable situation. Standing together in that musty room, we both realized that she had only two choices. She could either go back to an abusive spouse or she could live with the knowledge that not only were her children separated from her and one another, but that someone else was mothering them and tucking them into bed at night. I could offer her no words of wisdom or comfort. We just stood there and hugged each other, crying. About a week later, she chose what she felt was ultimately best for her children — temporary foster care.

As I drove home that cold winter afternoon where my own children were waiting for me in a house that was warm and well-lighted with plenty of room to spare, God left me no choice but to ask some painful questions about the system that had allowed this to happen to my student. I didn't like asking such questions, and I liked the answers even less, for I did not want to be part of the scene that was unfolding before me, any more than I wanted to be part of the crowd with blood on its hands this morning.

Where is my complicity in what happened to my student? I decided that afternoon that, in part, mine is a complicity of silence: Silence rather than advocacy for decent affordable childcare for all people. Silence rather than addressing the problem of gentrification that raises housing prices beyond the means of many. Silence rather than personal involvement leading to action about safety nets needed for all people who decide to leave such relationships.

My silence in not stepping back from the crowd this morning renders me just as much a part of the system that crucifies Jesus as my silence about the problems that emotionally crucified my student, for I am part of the crowd with blood on my hands, regardless of how much I wish it were not so.

Do you find yourself standing in the crowd with me? Where are you?

Wherever we may find ourselves, we must never forget that we are people of hope, redeemed through the power of the resurrection. I recently saw my student and she looked as content as I had ever seen her. She was pushing two children in one stroller and holding two others by the hand. She joyfully told me that she had moved in with a woman who took her to weekly Bible study and helped her with parenting, self-esteem, and high school equivalency classes. In addition, with the help of the Rev. Brian McCormick, director of Martin House, where I worked, she was now in an acceptable home with her four children.

Just as God did not desert Jesus on Calvary, God did not desert my student either. And just as God suffered with them and raised them to new glory, God can do the same for men and women who no longer want to be part of the crowd with blood on their hands.

For there really is a difference today. While we can't change what happened to Jesus *then*, we can change what happens to Jesus *now*. Why do unjust systems still crucify Jesus? Because earlier in Matthew's gospel Jesus states, "Truly I tell you, just as you did it to one of the least of these who are members of my family, you did it to me" (Matt. 25:40).

As we all know, it is the resurrection which is the final word on what happens in our narrative today. Similarly, it is the resurrection experience of my student which is the final word for her, and it is the possibility of resurrection for those of us standing in the crowd today that can be the final word for each one of us. Amen.

Yes, "For our sake he was crucified under Pontius Pilate." As I repeat these words, I am reminded of the women who stood at the foot of the cross on that hill on Calvary so long ago. I am reminded also of the Black women and women in developing nations today and throughout history who have identified with Jesus' suffering at the hands of an unjust system. In addition, I am painfully aware that I am part of the system that continues to crucify Jesus today, regardless of how much I wish it were not so.

Perhaps the remembering can help us struggle together for changes that are so desperately needed in our world today.

Christis depicted as a mother giving birth to the Church on the cross while a parallel is drawn to Eve's birth from the side of Adam.

MS. Bodl. 270b, fol. 6r detail from a *French Moralized Bible*, circa 1240.
Bodleian Library, Oxford, England.
Photo credit: Bodleian Library Imaging Services.

CHAPTER EIGHT

ON THE THIRD DAY HE ROSE AGAIN

C hristina Baxter, a contemporary Anglican theologian, states, "Jesus Christ's unity with God was not yet established by the claim implied in his appearance but only by his resurrection from the dead. . . The resurrection precipitates Christians into believing that Jesus Christ has an ontological identity with God."[1] The resurrection, which we affirm each time we recite the Nicene Creed, validates Jesus' pre-Easter message as having come directly from God. What was this pre-Easter message from God revealed to us through the life and ministry of Jesus Christ? Three of the four gospels record Jesus' first resurrection appearance as having been to a woman or women. Is it significant that this event, which lies at the center of our faith, is recorded as having been revealed first of all to women? Is this consonant with Jesus' pre-Easter message?

To answer these questions, it is helpful to begin with a brief overview of Jesus' relationship to women throughout his earthly ministry. Unlike other Jewish rabbis of his time, who reportedly also healed people, Jesus did heal women. It is significant that the first healing by Jesus recorded in the Gospel of Mark, the oldest gospel, is the healing of a woman, Simon Peter's mother-in-law (Mark 1:29-31; Matt. 8:14-15; Luke 4:38-39). In addition, all three of the synoptic gospels record Jesus' healing of the woman who had an issue of blood for twelve years. His willingness not only to touch the "unclean" woman but to call attention to the fact that he did so can only imply that he rejected the concept of the "uncleanness" of a woman who had a flow of blood (Mark 5:24-34; cf. Matt. 9:18-26; Luke 8:42-48). In another example, Jesus not only healed a woman on the Sabbath, he even called out to her in public, which was clearly against the rabbinic custom of his day. More amazing to this twentieth-century woman is that Luke records Jesus as referring to her as a "daughter of Abraham" (Luke 13:61a), an almost unheard of honorific in his day as well as in our own time, almost two thousand years later.

Furthermore, throughout Jesus' ministry he expressed concern for widows. Jesus publicly condemns the scribes for their oppression of widows (Mark 12:38-40; Luke 20:45-47). Additionally, Jesus flagrantly broke with the oppressive, patriarchal treatment of the women of his day through his actions in the following stories: the woman taken in adultery (John 8:2-11); the Samaritan woman at the well (John 4:1-42); Mary and Martha (Luke 10:38-42); and by the fact that all three synoptic gospels report that he had female disciples (Luke 8:1-3; cf. Mark 15:40-41; Matt. 27:55-56).[3]

In addition, one of the most important positions Jesus took in relation to the dignity of women concerned marriage. All three synoptic gospels record Jesus stating that in marriage women "had rights and responsibilities equal to men's" (see Mark 10:11-12; cf. Matt. 19:9; Luke 16:18).[4] In a similar vein, Jesus rejected the stereotype of his day of women as merely bearers of children. Rather, he insisted on their personhood and their intellectual and moral faculties as primary (Luke 11:27-28).[5]

It is no wonder that it was the women who stood at the foot of Jesus' cross while the men fled. It is no wonder that all four gospels also report them to have been the first to discover the empty tomb and/or to have encountered the risen Christ. What is wondrous is that even in the patriarchal culture in which these texts were written, three of the four gospels record the most important event of Jesus' ministry, his resurrection, as having been revealed first of all to women (Mark 16:9-11; Matt 28:8-10; John 20:11-18).

It should be noted that St. Paul does not refer to the resurrection appearance to St. Mary Magdalene in his earlier account in 1 Corinthians 15. Even so, Origen, who in the second century noted that "God does not stoop to look upon what is feminine and of the flesh"[6], nevertheless related this important first appearance to St. Mary Magdalene in defense of a stand taken by the second-century pagan philosopher, Celsus who remarked that the resurrection could not possibly have happened because "who saw this (the resurrection)? A hysterical female as you say ..." Origen responded, "There is no evidence of this (Mary Magdalene's hysteria) in the scriptural account (John 20:14-17) which was the source upon which he (Celsus) drew his criticism." Moreover, Origen noted that Matthew reports that the risen Jesus appeared to Mary Magdalene and another woman (Matt. 28:9-10).[7]

What then of St. Paul's omission in 1 Corinthians 15 of Jesus' appearance to St. Mary Magdalene? Some theologians comment that St. Paul states that Jesus first appeared to Cephas. However, a close inspection of the Greek text reveals that there is no word for "first" here. First Corinthians 15:5a has "and that he was seen by Cephas, then by the twelve." Well, it is true according to three of the gospel accounts that Jesus was in fact seen by Cephas and then by the Eleven, but according to three of the four gospels, he was seen by St. Mary Magdalene first. St. Paul adds no qualifying word here as to the position of the appearance to Peter except in relation to the other men. He merely omits the appearance to Mary. He does not state that it did not occur; nor does he claim that the appearance to Cephas was the first.

Not only do three of the four gospels report that Jesus first appeared to St. Mary Magdalene, they also record that she and the other women told the Eleven and others what they had seen. In keeping with the custom of the day, they were disbelieved, but they did evangelize the men nonetheless.

In the third century, Hippolytus of Rome wrote of Jesus

appearing first to St. Mary Magdalene and referred to her as an apostle and an evangelist.

Similarly, a well-known life of St. Mary Magdalene, written in the ninth century by Rabanus Maurus, states that Jesus commissioned her as an "apostle to the apostles." St. Bernard of Clairvaux also referred to St. Mary Magdalene as the "apostle to the apostles."[8]

It is disheartening that portions of scripture highlighting St. Mary Magdalene's role in witnessing to the apostles are either optional or omitted in the lectionary of the Episcopal Church. In "Lectionary Omissions," Jean Campbell writes: "For the principal service of Easter in Year A, John 21:1-18 is appointed with verses 11-18 optional. The optional verses from John contain the encounter between Mary Magdalene and the risen Lord with her subsequent proclamation to the disciples, "I have seen the Lord." In Year B, the Easter reading (Mk. 16:1-8) makes clear the fear of the women, but in Year C, Luke 24:1-20 omits verse 11, the one that recounts the disbelief of the disciples when the women proclaim that the tomb is empty and that they have been given a message."[9]

Because of these and other significant omissions, the lectionary is currently being studied by the Standing Liturgical Commission of the national Episcopal Church.

In Eastern Christian tradition, St. Mary Magdalene is credited with an even greater role in evangelizing than she is in the Western tradition. According to Eastern tradition, St. Mary Magdalene is believed to have journeyed to Rome after seeing the risen Christ. There she told Caesar what she had witnessed. "To explain this she picked up an egg from the table, whereupon Caesar protested that a human could no more rise from the dead than the egg in her hand could turn red. At once the egg turned blood red, which is why red eggs have been exchanged at Easter for centuries in the Byzantine East. Mary traveled the Mediterranean preaching the Resurrection and died a martyr like Peter and Paul" according to this tradition.[10]

In Western Christian tradition, St. Mary Magdalene also held a special position of honor. Because she was sent by

Jesus to witness to the male apostles, she was the only woman other than Jesus' mother on whose feast the Nicene Creed was recited.[11] Thus, St. Mary Magdalene as the apostle to the apostles, is historically linked with the reciting of the Nicene Creed.

Since three of the four gospels record the first resurrection appearances as having been made to a woman or women, it is logical to address the question of what this fact has to say about Jesus' (and therefore God's) intended message for the church. According to Leonard Swidler, Jesus is depicted as one learned in the Law, and therefore obviously aware of the stricture against women. The evangelists' description of Jesus' "first appearance to and commissioning of women to bear witness to the most important event of his career cannot be understood as anything but deliberate; it was a dramatic linking of a very clear rejection of the second-class status of women with the center of Jesus' gospel, his resurrection . . . It is an overwhelming tribute to man's (male) intellectual myopia not to have discerned it effectively in 2000 years."[12]

Black theologian James Cone, feminist theologian Anne Carr, and Latin American theologian Jon Sobrino all correctly point out that in his ministry Jesus consistently affirmed the outcast, the poor, and certainly women, who as half of the population, comprised a majority of the population of outcasts. Since the significance of the resurrection is that it renders Jesus as ontologically one with God, then we can only have here a clear mandate as to God's will regarding all of the oppressed, particularly women. By raising Jesus from the dead, God once and for all made it clear that Jesus' ministry was far more than the ministry of just one human being from Nazareth. Jesus' ministry with us was no less that the action of God on earth.

One can only conclude that God has spoken as to God's intended role for women. God has spoken through the actions of Jesus, time and again, against patriarchal structures that limit the freedom of women to be who they were created by God to be, in God's image.

What is more orthodox than such a mandate from scripture itself, as revealed in the life of Jesus of Nazareth? What is more orthodox than the fact of Jesus first appearing to St. Mary Magdalene when three gospels, Origen, Celsus, Rabanus Maurus, St. Bernard of Clairvaux, and others affirm the same? How can we acknowledge the boldness and sheer unlikelihood of this being the case without trying to discern the meaning behind it? As concerned Christians how can we fail to consider all of the evidence in the development of our understanding of the significance of the resurrection for us today?

As we recite the Nicene Creed and affirm our belief in the resurrection of the one Lord Jesus Christ, let us remember the women to whom Jesus chose to appear first. May those of us who struggle to be heard today remember that their witness, as recorded in three of the gospels, was viewed with skepticism when they first announced the good news that the risen Christ revealed to them.

When I state my belief that "On the third day he rose again in accordance with the Scriptures," with the knowledge of what this can mean for women, I am both affirmed and strengthened for the task that lies ahead.

PART III

But what is love or charity, which the divine Scripture praises and proclaims so highly, if not the love of the good? Now love is of someone who loves, and something is loved with love. So then there are three: the lover, the beloved, and the love.

St. Augustine of Hippo
Fifth Century

Detail of the top right panel from *Scenes from the Life of St. Augustine*, circa 1490, Master of St. Augustine.
The Metropolitan Museum of Art, The Cloisters Collection, New York (61.199).
Photo credit: The Photograph Library, The Metropolitan Museum of Art

CHAPTER NINE

WE BELIEVE IN
THE HOLY SPIRIT

The third article of the Nicene Creed begins, "We believe in the Holy Spirit, the Lord, the giver of life." Designations of the Holy Spirit as "Lord" and "giver of life" in the creed are of immense theological importance to a correct understanding of the identity of the Spirit.

The Holy Spirit as "the giver of life", is in keeping with Johannine theology in which the Holy Spirit is the agent of our second birth. We are born from the womb of the Spirit. In John 3:4-5, Nicodemus asks Jesus, "'Can one enter a second time into the mother's womb and be born?' Jesus answered, 'Very truly, I tell you, no one can enter the kingdom of God without being born of water and the Spirit.'"

Thus, the Spirit is indeed the source of life. Creation of new life through the Holy Spirit is articulated and lived out in the Christian community every time a person is baptized. The baptized one puts on the clothes of Christ, but it is the power of the Holy Spirit that enables believers to clothe themselves in this heavenly garment.

The rite of Holy Baptism in the Episcopal Church's *1979 Book of Common Prayer* articulates this reality and traces the connection between water and the Holy Spirit back to the beginning of creation, through the crossing of the Red Sea, into a Johannine understanding of the Holy Spirit.

The Prayer Book states, "We thank you, Almighty God, for the gift of water. Over it the Holy Spirit moved in the beginning of creation. Through it you led the children of Israel out of their bondage in Egypt into the land of promise. In it your Son Jesus received the baptism of John and was anointed by the Holy Spirit as the Messiah, the Christ, to lead us, through his death and resurrection, from the bondage of sin into everlasting life. We thank you, Father, for the water of Baptism. In it we are buried with Christ in his death. By it we share in his resurrection. Through it we are reborn by the Holy Spirit."[1]

Thus, the Holy Spirit is the agent not only of our second birth, but of our first birth and all life on earth, for the Holy Spirit moved over water in the beginning of creation (Gen. 1:1-2). The passage through water, from bondage, into the promised land parallels the birth process — out of the bondage of the womb, through the waters of birth, into new life. Then when there is a need for reconciliation, people are reborn in the Spirit, again through water.

Isn't the connection between the Holy Spirit, birth, and water an unmistakably feminine one? The Hebrew word *ruach*, which means "spirit" is feminine, reflecting this understanding. The Greek word *pneuma*, which means "spirit", is neuter, but in Greek all of the gifts associated with the spirit are feminine in gender.[2] The Latin word for spirit, *spiritus*, is masculine, but even though some church fathers wrote in this language, it is not as operative as the Hebrew and Greek words, since it is in these two languages that the scriptures were written.

When we look at the Hebrew and Greek words for spirit and for those gifts associated with it, along with the consistent imagery of the Holy Spirit as the agent of birth, a birth that must occur through water, a strong case can be made for the Spirit as having feminine attributes.

In *She Who Is*, Elizabeth Johnson links these feminine aspects of the Spirit with the neglect of the Holy Spirit in later Christian theology. Whereas the Holy Spirit was the focus of theological discourse in the second century by Irenaeus, in the third century by Origen and Tertullian, and in the fourth century by St. Basil and St. Athanasius, later theologians have neglected to focus on the Holy Spirit. She writes:

In recent years the theory has grown that one of the key if unarticulated reasons for the tradition's forgetfulness of the Spirit lies precisely here, in the alliance between the idea of Spirit and the roles and persons of actual women marginalized in church and society . . . In the Bible the Spirit's work includes bringing forth and nurturing life, holding all things together, and constantly renewing what the ravages of time and sin break down. This is surely analogous to traditional "women's work", . . . Neglect of the Spirit and the marginalizing of women have a symbolic affinity and may well go hand in hand.[3]

English psychologist Janet Sayers, author of *Sexual Contradictions*, provides a possible explanation for the marginalizing of women when she describes the phenomenon of men's envy of women as "womb envy."[4] To support her position, she quotes pioneering psychologist Karen Horney, who wrote in 1926 that "when one begins, as I did, to analyze men only after a fairly long experience of analyzing women, one receives a most surprising impression of the intensity of this envy of pregnancy, childbirth, and motherhood."[5]

Feminist scholars in the fields of anthropology, history, philosophy, and theology concur. There is an emerging consensus among them that patriarchy "arose as a compensation for men's physiological inability to give birth. In early societies, giving birth connoted a divine power especially when the male role in procreation was not yet known. Females, in being able to reproduce themselves, exhibited greater permanence and were experienced as having the key to immortality in a way that males did not."[6] Thus, to achieve a position of power, the male was moved to dominate the woman's sexuality and reproductive capacity in a way that the female became the private property of the male, thus giving rise to the patriarchal system.[7]

Similarly, Adrienne Rich writes that men's attitudes of dominance towards women are based in part on their deep-rooted desire to compensate themselves for their envy of women's power in bearing and rearing children.[8]

The fact that some women are more likely to be battered by spouses or boyfriends during pregnancy may support this assertion. In *Wife Beating: The Silent Crisis*, Roger Langley and Richard Levy note that pregnancy is a change that often brings on spouse abuse and state that violence occurs during pregnancy in almost 25 percent of the families who report violence.[9]

Thus, the woman as "the giver of life" can cause resent- ment among some men. The Holy Spirit as giver of life through water is unmistakably a feminine image. Catholic theologian Elizabeth Johnson postulates that for this rea- son the Holy Spirit has been devalued throughout the his- tory of Christian theology, just as women have been deval- ued throughout the history of humankind.

In asserting that the Holy Spirit as giver of life is a femi- nine image, it must be stated unequivocally that whereas the Holy Spirit is associated with feminine attributes, it does not mean that the Holy Spirit is feminine any more than the first and second persons of the Trinity are eternally and essentially masculine. When theology is articulated in human language within a patriarchal framework, such gen- der designation results. Yet such designation is inadequate to the theology that underlies the Nicene Creed.

Why? In part, because the creed states: "We believe in the Holy Spirit, the Lord." Through this immediate desig- nation of the Holy Spirit as "the Lord," the Spirit is linked with both God and Jesus Christ. As discussed in Chapters II and IV, both God and Jesus Christ can be regarded as eternally and essentially beyond gender distinction.

God is referred to as "Lord", or *kurios*, numerous times throughout Hebrew scripture and the New Testament. Jesus refers to himself as *kurios* only once, in a passage in both Matthew and Mark (Mark 11:3, Matt 21:3). However, Jesus was addressed as *kurios* much more frequently. Furthermore, in seven places in the New Testament it is not clear whether God or Christ is meant by the word *kurios*.[10]

The designation of the Holy Spirit as "Lord" means that the Holy Spirit is equal to God. *Confessing the One Faith* states: "In using the title 'Lord' for the Holy Spirit . . . the Creed affirms that the Spirit's divinity is *exactly* that of the Father and the Son."[11] Although St. Paul says "Now the Lord is the Spirit" (2 Cor 3:17), it was not until after much debate that this clause was included in the Nicene Creed of 381.

Just as the Arian controversy produced a debate about the nature of Christ at the Council of Nicea in 325, so too it produced a parallel debate about the Being of the Holy Spirit. This time St. Athanasius, in about 360, found himself addressing the Bishop of Thomius, who argued that if the Spirit were of God, then it must be another Son. Since the Son is only-begotten, the Son can have no brother. Thus, the bishop argued, the Spirit must be a Grandson of God the Father.[12] Whereas this may seem comical to us today, isn't it a natural outgrowth of human, hierarchical, paternalistic language when used in relation to the Triune God? In response to the Bishop of Thomius, St. Athanasius argued that the Spirit is the spirit of Christ within each one of us. Thus, the divinity of the Spirit is equal to Christ's divinity.[13]

Ten to fifteen years after St. Athanasius, St. Basil of Caesarea wrote: "The Lord has delivered to us a necessary and saving dogma: the Holy Spirit is to be ranked with the Father."[14] Further, "in everything the Holy Spirit is indivisibly and inseparably joined to the Father and the Son" and "the Holy Spirit partakes of the fullness of divinity."[15]

These views set forth by St. Athanasius and St. Basil resulted in the Holy Spirit being ranked equal in glory and worship with God and Jesus in the Nicene Creed of 381. This equality was also affirmed in the liturgy of the early church. According to Frances Young, "In its liturgy, the (early) church accorded equal honour and dignity to Son and Spirit as to the Father, which was appropriate since all shared the same divine nature, and all were involved in the divine activities of creation and salvation."[16]

This view is echoed in the Thirty-Nine Articles of Religion, written by the Church of England in response to controversies of the sixteenth century. Article Five maintains: "The Holy Ghost, proceeding from the Father and the Son, is of *one substance*, majesty, and glory, with the Father and the Son, very and eternal God."[17] Here we see divinity predicated of the Holy Spirit in the same way that the Nicene Creed predicates of the Son, one substance or *homoousios*.

The Nicene Creed declares, "With the Father and the Son he is worshiped and glorified." Like the designation of the Spirit as "Lord," this phrase underscores the equality of the Spirit with the Father and the Son, but here by predication of equal worship and glory.

The use of the pronoun "he" here, which is not in the original Greek text and not linguistically necessary, perpetuates a theological inaccuracy each time it is repeated, since the Holy Spirit is not masculine, any more than the first and second persons of the Trinity are eternally and essentially masculine. This is undoubtedly why in the original text of the Nicene Creed, only neuter articles are used to describe the third person of the Trinity. No masculine articles are used in reference to the Holy Spirit yet the English translation inserts them.

The fact that all three persons of the Trinity are of one substance and without body, and are therefore eternally and essentially beyond gender distinction, is succinctly stated in the first article of the Thirty-Nine Articles. Article One says: "There is but one living and true God, everlasting, *without body*, parts, or passions; of infinite power, wisdom and goodness; the Maker and Preserver of all things both visible and invisible. And in unity of this Godhead there be *three Persons, of one substance*, power, and eternity; the Father, the Son, and the Holy Ghost."[18]

In an explication of Article One, E.J. Bicknell writes:

> The perversion of the truth of the personality of God is known as "anthropomorphism." We fall into this error when we ascribe to God the limitations and imperfections of our own finite human personalities. Anthropomorphism degrades the idea of God by ascribing to Him human infirmities . . . By speaking of God as "everlasting" (*aeternus*) and "without body," we mean that God is raised above the limitations of both time and space.[19]

What I find problematic is the anthropomorphism supported by some contemporary theologians. In *Speaking the Christian God: The Holy Trinity and the Challenge of Feminism*, Elizabeth Achtemeier asserts: "If we ask 'What is the ontological nature of God?' we must reply 'God is the Father of Jesus Christ.'"[20] Alvin Kimel maintains that "God is not just like a father; he is *the* Father. Jesus is not just like a son; he is *the* Son. The divine Fatherhood and Sonship are absolute, transcendent, and correlative."[21]

How can God's fatherhood be viewed as ontological, that is, as of the very being of God, when God clearly transcends sexuality or gender? In the same essay, Achtemeier even states: "It is universally recognized by biblical scholars that the God of the Bible has no sexuality."[22] If so, how can God ontologically be Father?

In *The Doctrine of the Trinity*, Leonard Hodgson maintains: "In orthodox Christian theology God is not a person, so that it is more accurate to speak of personality *in* than *of* God."[23] Thus, God is beyond the limits of personhood, beyond the limits of fatherhood. It is for this reason that one image of God can never contain the glory that is God.

If the three persons are of one substance, or *ousia*, and the one substance is without body, as the first of the Thirty-Nine Articles states, *then all three persons of the Trinity must of necessity be eternally and essentially beyond gender distinctions. Asserting that any of the three persons is essentially and eternally gender-bound is theologically inaccurate and against the underlying theology of the Nicene Creed.*

On this point, Bicknell writes: "The West retained *Una substantia, Tres Personae*. So it comes that in English we speak about 'Three Persons in One Substance,' a literal translation of the Latin. The English terms are not altogether happy. They convey false associations that are absent from the Greek."[24] Further,

> owing to the fact that human persons walk about in bodies divided by space, it is hard to free our imagination from the idea of separation in connexion with (the English word) "Person." So, too, "substance" to our ears suggests the occupation of space. The terms need explanation . . . All theologians confess that the best (Trinitarian) language that can be found is inadequate. The Church only uses these words, because she cannot escape . . . The (church) Fathers are full

of similar confessions of the inadequacy of human language. The Church does not claim to be able to define or explain all that Godhead means. All that is taught is that whatever Godhead means, *all three Persons equally possess it.*[25]

This equality is asserted in the Nicene Creed which states that the Son is *homoousios* or of 'one substance' with the Father. In stating that Jesus is *homoousios* with God it is helpful to distinguish between Jesus' substance, or *ousia*, and his person, or *hypostasis,* as discussed in chapter IV. Jesus' Jewishness and maleness belong to his person, or *hypostasis*. His substance, or *ousia*, belongs to the universal and is therefore not bound by gender restrictions. Understanding the distinction between Christ's person and substance is important not only for women, but for all non-Jews in their inclusion in Christ's humanity. For this reason Christ is referred to as having "impersonal humanity."[26]

The creed then affirms that the Holy Spirit is "Lord" and is "worshiped and glorified with the Father and the Son." "The Creed does not use, as does later theology, the term *homoousios* to describe the identity of the Holy Spirit in relation to God the Father . . . In using the title 'Lord' for the Holy Spirit, however, the Creed affirms that the Spirit's divinity is exactly that of the Father and the Son which was defended through the use of the term *homoousios*."[27] Thus, all three persons of the Trinity must of necessity be eternally and essentially free of gender restrictions.

The ICET translation of the Creed says of the Holy Spirit, "He has spoken through the Prophets." The ELLC has replaced "he" with "who" in this phrase, which is more in accordance with the theology of the Holy Spirit as reflected in the creed itself. Since the Holy Spirit, like God and Christ, is not essentially gender-bound, "who" is a more appropriate pronoun to use than "he." It is also indisputably a more accurate translation of the original Greek text, which uses only neuter articles in describing the third person of the Trinity.

The prophets spoken of in this passage are those prophets who spoke in the name of God before the Bible was written, within the biblical writings, and up to the composition of the creed itself. They include Miriam, sister of Moses, who helped lead the Israelites in the exodus journey (Exod. 15:20); Deborah, one of the Israelite leaders during the time of the judges (Judges 4:4ff); Huldah, who was consulted by five people, including the priest Hilkiah (2 Kings 22:14); and the unnamed woman who is called a prophet by Isaiah (Isa. 8:3)[28], who also wrote of God as a woman in labor, gasping and panting (42:14), a comforting mother (66:13f), and a compassionate mother (49:14-16). It includes Hosea, who describes God as a mother feeding a suckling child (11:1-4) and a mother bear protecting her cubs (13:8).

I pray for the day when all of the biblical prophets are honored and all of the prophetic images of God are heard, inwardly digested, and manifested in the liturgy and teaching of the contemporary church.

The Trinity

In asserting that the Father, Son, and Holy Spirit are co-equal, the Nicene Creed articulates a trinitarian understanding of God. Although the Trinity is not mentioned outright, the three articles of the creed clearly support a trinitarian view of God. As such, a brief discussion of the trinity is in order here.

A fifteenth-century Flemish painting in the series "Scenes from the Life of Augustine," reproduced on page 68, depicts a boy sitting on the beach. He has dug a hole in the sand and is trying to fill it with water. St. Augustine, as legend has it, says to the boy, "Young man, don't you realize what you're attempting is an impossible task?" The boy replies, "Don't you realize that trying to write about the Trinity is an impossible task?"

In recognizing that I am attempting the impossible, I nonetheless begin my dig in the sand.

We should start by remembering that we are undertaking our task in the last decade of the twentieth century. As such, we have the collected wisdom of almost two thousand years of Christian theological reflection. Some contemporary theologians choose to forget this fact and instead insist on a much earlier view of the Trinity, a view circumscribed by an earlier time and culture. While this view is classical, for theological reflection today to be stuck in the early centuries is not in the tradition of the classical theologians. Leonard Hodgson writes: *"If we are to be true successors of the classical theologians, we must try to think as honestly in the terms of the thought of today as they did in those of their time."*[29]

There are basically two different ways of approaching a discussion of the doctrine of the Trinity — the economic Trinity and the immanent Trinity. These two views are different ways of talking about God, not different ways of God being God.

An economic understanding of the Trinity is "the Trinity as revealed by God's threefold dealing with men (sic). God had made Himself known through the life of Christ and the coming of the Spirit as Creator, Redeemer and Sanctifier."[30] Kenneth Cauthen states that in the economic Trinity "the three persons of the Trinity refer to the different ways we experience God."[31] On the other hand, the immanent Trinity, sometimes referred to as the essential or social Trinity, describes "the relations of the Three Persons as they are to one another in the eternal life of God."[32] In the immanent Trinity, the three persons are eternal and internal distinctions within the being of God. The emphasis is on the way the three persons exist in relation to one another.[33]

The doctrine of the immanent Trinity has been critiqued by Catherine LaCugna in *God For Us*: The doctrine of the immanent Trinity became concerned with only "the intradivine relationality of God to God, thought of apart from the relationship of God *to us* through Jesus Christ and the Holy Spirit."[34] Such a view of the Trinity leaves out you and me and the entire created order, thereby rendering it an inadequate formulation of trinitarian doctrine.

LaCugna favors an economic Trinity in which the focus is on the different ways God relates to us. With such an understanding of the Trinity, there is revealed the "unfathomable mystery that the life and communion of the divine persons is not 'intradivine': God is not self-contained, egotistical and self-absorbed but overflowing love, outreaching desire for union with all that God has made. The communion of divine life is God's communion *with us* in Christ and as Spirit."[35]

In thus favoring the concept of the economic Trinity, LaCugna critiques Patricia Wilson-Kastner's focus on the immanent Trinity as *perichoresis* which LaCugna defines as "the idea that the three divine persons mutually inhere in one another, draw life from one another, 'are' what they are by relation to one another. *Perichoresis* means being-in-one-another, permeation without confusion."[36]

The word *perichoresis* literally means a dance round or dancing together.[37] Of this understanding of the Trinity, Wilson-Kastner states: "The divine trinitarian dance is a far more appealing, inclusive, and revealing sign of the divine than the two seated white males and a dove, or a divine unity, male or female in image."[38] Thus, Wilson-Kastner puts relationality at the very heart of God.

Of this view of the Trinity, LaCugna says, "While *perichoresis* is appealed to as theological justification for the values of mutuality, equality and reciprocity, this trinitarian interrelatedness takes place *in divinis*, at the level of intratrinitarian relations."[39]

While I believe LaCugna is correct in her point about *perichoresis*, I find her conclusions to be disappointing. The doctrine of the Trinity, she says, "succeeds when it illumines God's nearness to us in Christ and the Spirit. But it fails if the divine persons are imprisoned in an intradivine realm."[40] Further, "there is only one sure basis for a Christian theology of God, namely, the communion of *God with us* in the economy of redemption."[41]

Why must this be an either/or proposition? Isn't both an immanent and an economic view of the Trinity appropriate?

To focus purely on God's interrelatedness is to miss a significant part of who God is. But to focus purely on God's relationship to us, as LaCugna suggests, is also limiting. Why? Because in focusing on God as only in relation to the created order, we leave out the eternalness of God. What is the nature of God's being if not intradivine reality? Is it not putting ourselves at the center, rather than God, when we state that God's trinitarian nature can only be expressed in terms of us? Is this where the current focus on "the self" has led us?

I agree with LaCugna that correct trinitarian understanding must include God's relationship with us, but God's being is not dependent on us. God is God from before time and into the ages of ages.

Thus, I believe that a correct trinitarian understanding should include both an economic and an immanent understanding of the nature of the trinitarian God. I agree with Jürgen Moltmann and Karl Rahner, who state that "the economic Trinity is the immanent Trinity, and vice versa."[42]

Moltmann justifies this position in *The Trinity and the Kingdom.*

> The meaning of the cross of the Son on Golgotha reaches right into the heart of the immanent Trinity. From the very beginning, no immanent Trinity and no divine glory is conceivable without "the Lamb who was slain" . . . On the cross God *creates* salvation outwardly for his whole creation and at the same time *suffers* this disaster of the whole world inwardly in himself . . . What this thesis is actually trying to bring out is the interaction between the substance and the revelation, the 'inwardness' and the "outwardness" of the triune God. The economic Trinity not only reveals the immanent Trinity; it also has a retroactive effect on it.[43]

Thus, an immanent Trinity is necessary to understand God's eternalness as well as God's intradivine nature. As God effected our salvation through the cross, God's internal being was also affected, according to Moltmann and Rahner. Thus, it is impossible to discuss an economic Trinity without understanding that it has a retroactive effect on the immanent Trinity. Therefore, a both/and approach to Trinitarian theology is the most appropriate.

I would now like to turn to the issue of trinitarian language. First, as discussed by theologians throughout the Christian tradition, in an economic Trinity, God is described as Trinity because we relate to God in three different ways. It is through these ways of relating that God has been revealed throughout salvation history. Karl Barth starts with this affirmation of Trinitarian doctrine. He feels that the Trinity implies a "Revealer (the Father), a Revelation (the Son), and Revealedness (the Spirit)."[44] St. Thomas Aquinas also felt that "the doctrine of the Trinity expresses a truth known to us only by Divine revelation."[45] Leonard Hodgson concurs. "It (the Trinity) could not have been discovered by reason apart from that revelation."[46]

An understanding of God based on revelation must be based on a belief in progressive revelation. This allows trinitarian doctrine to keep pace with orthodoxy, for orthodoxy is not fixed and unchangeable for all time. Rather, it is subject to progressive revelations throughout history.

This is where I, as a human, encounter a problem with traditional trinitarian language. With the Trinity described only in terms of Father, Son, and Holy Spirit, part of God's self-revelation in scripture and throughout the Christian tradition is not included. Does our exclusive use of the formula Father, Son, and Holy Spirit really allow for all of the richness and complexity that lie just below the surface of the Nicene Creed?

For Catherine LaCugna, an exception to the desire to expand trinitarian language is the case of the baptismal formula. She supports keeping the Father-Son language in the baptismal formula for ecumenical reasons and concludes that "it is unnecessary to repudiate the baptismal formula as inherently sexist and patriarchal."[47]

In keeping with this understanding, the 1991 General Convention of the Episcopal Church passed resolution B033A, which states: "That the 70th General Convention of the Episcopal Church reaffirm its insistence upon baptism with water in the Triune Name of God: Father, Son, and Holy Spirit."[48]

An alternative that might satisfy this resolution but would also be inclusive is the formula "in the name of the Father, and of the Son, and of the Holy Spirit, one God Mother of us all."[49] These words would preserve the trinitarian formula and yet also acknowledge the feminine aspects of our creator.

In places where the Trinity is used other than for baptism, LaCugna writes, "It is crucial that liturgical, pastoral, and systematic theologians continue to explore new ways of addressing God in public prayer. While changes in language, especially liturgical language, are not cosmetic, at the same time there is ample precedent for making emendations for the sake of worship *and* for the sake of better conforming to contemporary experience . . . Language that hurts or language that excludes or language that legitimates the subordination of any group should be changed."[50]

As precedent for liturgical change she cites Basil's change in the fourth century in the great doxology from its original form, "to the Father, through the Son, in the Holy Spirit," to the form "to the Father with the Son and with the Holy Spirit."[51]

In addition, it is an injustice to God's self-revelation to limit the Trinity to only one language. Karl Barth states that "the Trinity is the immediate implication of revelation."[52] If the Trinity is the immediate implication of revelation, then shouldn't trinitarian language reflect the diversity and complexity of that revelation? There is a reason why biblical writers and the early church fathers use a constellation of images for God, Jesus, and the Holy Spirit. Why is it that only one image is used whenever we speak liturgically of God in trinitarian language?

One of my own favorite images of the Trinity dates to the fifth century. In *De Trinitate*, St. Augustine writes that "love itself is a substance itself worthy of the name of God, and not merely because it is a gift of God."[53] He states further that all love involves the trinity of lover, beloved, and love, yet he does not treat this as trinitarian analogy. "But what is love or charity, which the divine Scripture praises and proclaims so highly, if not the love of the good? Now love is of someone who loves, and something is loved with love. So then there are three: the lover, the beloved, and the love."[54]

Within the trinitarian designation of Lover, Beloved,

and Love, can both an immanent and an economic Trinity be embraced? This *perichoretic* image is clearly one of an immanent Trinity, for it exists at the level of God's intradivine nature. It embraces the way God relates internally. It is also clearly an economic designation. for what revelation is more biblical than the revelation that God is love? God tells the people of Israel, "I have loved you with an everlasting love" (Jeremiah 31:3). John 3:16 states, "For God so loved the world that he gave his only begotten son," while St. Paul assures us, "For I am convinced that neither death, nor life, nor angels, nor rulers, nor things present, nor things to come, nor powers, nor height, nor depth, nor anything else in all creation, will be able to separate us from the love of God in Christ Jesus our Lord" (Rom. 8:38-39).

Furthermore, what is more central to God's revelation through Jesus than the revelation that Jesus is God's beloved? At the baptism of Jesus, the heavens open and a voice says, "You are my Son, the Beloved, with you I am well pleased" (Mark 1:11; Luke 3:22; Matt. 3:17). This designation of Jesus as the Beloved appears in all three synoptic gospels with almost identical wording.

In addition, what is more central to scripture and Christian theology than the understanding that the Holy Spirit is love? St. Gregory, in his Homily XXX on Pentecost writes, "The Holy Ghost Himself is Love."[55] Aquinas comments, "The name Love in God can be taken essentially and personally. If taken personally it is the proper name of the Holy Ghost."[56] Poets throughout history have made similar affirmations. In his poem "Christus," Henry Wadsworth Longfellow writes: "Love is the Holy Ghost within."[57]

According to Patricia Wilson-Kastner, "Love is not simply one factor among others in the dynamic of the universe itself and its relationship to God. It is the essence of the issue, the fundamental self-revelation of God, and the basic energy in which all holds together."[58]

When we enter into relationship with the Lover, the Beloved, and the Love that exists between them, we are encircled by an eternal, all-encompassing love. Caught up in this whirl of triune Love, how can we escape the very real understanding that God loves us with a love that is beyond description and knows no boundaries? It is this love that enables us to become Lovers of Souls ourselves. It is this love that enables us to believe that indeed, we are the beloved. It is this love that has the power to transform lives and the world in which we live.

The trinitarian designation of God as Lover, Beloved, and Love embraces both God's intradivine nature and the primary way God as Trinity relates to us. The primary revelation of God throughout scripture is that God is love. Thus, it is consistent with God's revelation to us. In addition, it moves beyond gender-designated language which restricts the ability of many to realize that God is truly beyond gender, beyond any human language. It enables both women and men to feel that they are caught up in the triune love that is the mystery of God.

I am not suggesting that this language *replace* current Father, Son, and Holy Spirit language. I do suggest that it be *added to it*. Again, it is an issue of both/and rather than either/or. Let there be established in every subdivision of the churches a committee to consider this question and to propose alternatives to be discussed in regional meetings and used in the liturgy or worship of the churches.

Yes, we believe in one God; in one Lord, Jesus Christ, who is of one being with the Father; and in the Holy Spirit, the Lord who is worshiped and glorified. In making this assertion, I am proclaiming my belief in these three persons of the Trinity who are all eternally and essentially beyond gender distinctions.

When our trinitarian language can move beyond gender designation, only then can the fullness of God's revelation more adequately be included. Then everyone, male and female alike, can find themselves caught up in the triune love that is God.

What gifts the creed does indeed hold for those, who as Evelyn Underhill says, "take the trouble to dig below the surface, and seek for the Treasure which is still hidden in the field."[59]

CHAPTER TEN

ONE HOLY CATHOLIC AND APOSTOLIC CHURCH

As the third article of the Nicene Creed continues, there is a notable shift in emphasis. The focus is no longer on things ethereal; it is, rather, a "discussion of what is lowest, nearest, most actual, namely ourselves," states Karl Barth.[1] If you feel that the creed bears little relevance to your life today, you may want to reflect on these last phrases of the Nicene Creed.

What does it mean to us as Christians to be part of "one holy catholic and apostolic Church"? To answer that question, it is helpful to define the word *church*. In doing so, most people envision a church building or clergy. Yet Archbishop Trevor Huddleston states: "In the Bible, out of all the chapters and verses where the word occurs, only *once* (and that is in the Old Testament) does it refer to a building. The original word, first in Hebrew, then in Greek and Latin, means 'called' — or rather — 'called out.' The Church in which we are professing our belief is always people . . . people who are 'called out' by God for a purpose."[2]

Similarly, theologian Hans Küng writes: "Certainly the Church is always more than the sum of its individual members; but it is and remains the fellowship of its believing members, which God has gathered into his people. There can be no Church without this people of believers. We are the Church — not God, not Christ, not the Spirit. Without us and outside us the Church has no reality."[3] Further, he affirms that as the church we are called out:

> If the Church really sees itself as the people of God, it is obvious that it can never be a static and supra-historical phenomenon, which exists undisturbed by earthly space and historical time. The Church is always and everywhere a living people, gathered together from the peoples of this world and journeying through the midst of time. The Church is essentially *en route*, on a journey, a pilgrimage.[4]

On this pilgrimage, as members of the holy catholic church, we are called out beyond the walls of our own churches, our own communities, our own countries to be the church in the world. We don't go to church; we are the church.

In addition to the image of the Church as the people of God, other images are used to describe the church in the New Testament, such as vine, temple, bride, the new Jerusalem. Yet *Confessing the One Faith* states that no image is so predominant as the image of the church as the body of Christ.[5] As St. Paul tells us: "Now you are the body of Christ and individually members of it" (1 Cor. 12:27).

Yes, we are the church in the world. We are the body of Christ in the world, and that body is holy, catholic, and apostolic.

What does it mean to say that the church as the people of God, the body of Christ, is holy? It does not mean that the people in the church are individually holy. Individual members are in need of justification and sanctification. Hans Küng writes, "It is God who sanctifies the Church. Men [sic] in the Church are not, any more than men [sic] in the world, holy of themselves."[6] It is, in fact, because individual Christians, beginning in the New Testament, are called to be holy, that they are themselves called holy.

This is an important distinction that needs to be taught in the church. Many times I have talked with disillusioned parishioners who tell me, "I somehow thought people in the church wouldn't be like everyone else. But they are. So what's the point in being part of the church?"

We must remember that it is God who makes the church holy, through the power of the Holy Spirit. It is belief that God can do this that unites us as a Christian body. Belief in the church is under the category of belief in the Holy Spirit. It is not just that we believe in the church; it is belief in the spirit-filled church, the church to which the Holy Spirit gave birth.

Holy means set apart. The church is holy in that it is set apart to do God's work on earth. In making this assertion, it is important to remember that the church is not set apart *from* the world but *in* the world. Hans Küng maintains:

> The Church presses forward, set apart from the world, different from the other communities of the world . . . And yet this community which has been set apart must not cut itself off from the world . . . the Church has not been simply taken out of the world, it has been sent back into the world as something holy, belonging to God.[7]

In addition to being holy, the Church is catholic in the sense that it is universal. The universal church is meant to be all-inclusive, to be for everyone. The oneness of the church in fact establishes the imperative for ecumenical relations today. This is creedal theology. There is, therefore, an imperative about ecumenism.

In addition, *Confessing the One Faith* states: "Its catholicity means that it [the church] is the gift of God for all people whatever their particular country, race, social condition or language."[8] As St. Paul writes, "There is no longer Jew or Greek, there is no longer slave or free, there is no longer male and female; for all of you are one in Christ Jesus" (Gal. 3:28).

For the church to be truly catholic it must be for all; everyone must be able to participate in each aspect of the life of the church. This includes men and women; African Americans, Euro-Americans, Native Americans, Asians, and Latinos; young and old, gay and straight, rich and poor. All come within the reach of God's saving embrace. All are meant to be part of a church that is both holy and catholic.

Being the church, the body of Christ, in the world means that we do not close our eyes to the genuine injustice, pain, and suffering of others. For as St. Paul tells us, "If one member (of the body) suffers, all suffer together with it; if one member is honored, all rejoice together with it" (I Cor. 12:26).

Have you found this to be true in your Christian community? If not, how might your life be different if it were true?

It is important to note that within the women's movement itself, feelings have been expressed that not all members are suffering together. The movement has been criticized by women of color for having a predominantly white, educated agenda. In *Ain't I a Woman*, bell hooks writes:

> Initially, black feminists approached the women's movement white women had organized eager to join the struggle to end sexist oppression. We were disappointed and disillusioned when we discovered that white women in the movement had little knowledge of or concern for the problems of lower class and poor women or the particular problems of non-white women from all classes.[9]

Working in the inner city for four years with women of color, I experienced first-hand the differences in our needs. Daily survival in drug-infested neighborhoods where there is not enough food or housing for everyone is not part of my daily life in suburbia. Had I not chosen to work in the inner city, such realities would have been little more than statistics in the newspapers or a story on the six o'clock news to me.

Yet being a member of the holy catholic church means that we are called out from our comfortable lives to share in the joy and pain of others. As a result, the issues of all women throughout the world are our issues as are the issues of all men and children throughout the world as well.

The Rev. Dr. Carter Heyward echoes this sentiment in her address given at the World-wide Anglican Encounter in Brazil. She stated that hopefulness can no longer disregard "the violence, poverty, terror, and confusion in our lives and those of our sisters. For any *hope* that denies the massive suffering of the world . . . is no hope at all."[10]

Through first-hand experience I am aware of the need for such universal hopefulness by women living in the inner cities of our own country. Through travel and reading I am aware of the needs of women outside the United States.

On a recent trip to England, several friends and I were sharing a taxi. As we rode, they asked about my clerical clothes and what kinds of vestments I wore at the altar. Then my friends got out of the cab and I continued to a further destination.

At this point, the driver turned to me and asked incredulously, "Are you a woman priest?" "Yes," I replied. "I'm orthodox," he offered, "and in our church women are not even allowed to take communion when they are having their period. Yet, you celebrate communion!" he said accusingly.

I was shocked, not only at his words to me, a stranger, but at the content of what he was saying. I did not know that some women in the Christian faith in first-world countries today are denied communion when they are menstruating.

"Why are they denied communion at such times? I can't believe that!" I blurted out. "Because it's the body and blood of Christ!" he stated emphatically.

My mind went to the story of Jesus, healing the unclean woman who had an issue of blood for twelve years (Matt 9:20-22; Mark 5:24-34; Luke 8:43-48). I wondered what Jesus must think. I wondered how the women must feel.

Yet even this kind of overt oppression can seem minor when compared to the oppression of women in developing nations. In a paper delivered at the Ninth Biennial Conference of the Evangelical Women's Caucus in July 1990, Rosemary Radford Ruether related that tens of thousands of women in India have died or been severely injured in dowry murders or attempted murders. Once the dowry has been delivered, along with the bride, "kitchen accidents are contrived to burn her to death. The groom and his family then go looking for another bride."[11]

Another testimony to the appalling treatment of women in developing nations is related in Alice Walker's *Possessing the Secret of Joy*, which tells the heart-rending story of Tashi, an African woman who marries an African-American man, Adam, and comes to America. First, however, she is circumcised, and thereby rendered unable to walk except by shuffling.

In the conclusion, Walker states that from ninety to one hundred million girls and women living today in African, Middle Eastern, and Far Eastern countries have suffered some form of circumcision or mutilation. "Recent articles in the media have reported on the growing practice of 'female circumcision' in the United States and Europe, among immigrants from countries where it is part of the culture."[12]

A recent *New York Times* article by A.M. Rosenthal states: "Every year millions of African girls and some Asians, are mutilated (circumcised). About 80 million now live with scars on their bodies and minds. Nobody can know how many more millions died from the mutilations — or the diseases to which their bodies were exposed by them . . . In America, the capture of Chinese refugees received more press and Congressional scrutiny over a few days than the mutilation of millions of women has attracted over decades."[13] How can this fact be reality in our world today?

We live in a world in which tens of thousands of women are burned or murdered for dowry rights, millions of women are routinely circumcised, some women are denied communion if they are menstruating, and others barely survive the triple effects of sexism, racism, and classism. And this list just scratches the surface.

Oppression of these groups of women is part of a larger whole. How can we as caring Christians fail to speak out with whatever gifts and inclinations God has given us?

Whether the oppression is expressed linguistically, doctrinally, through policy, or through accepted social practice, it still denigrates half of the human race. In so doing, is it not all of the human race that is denigrated, male and female alike? "If one member suffers, all suffer together with it" (1 Cor. 12:26).

Not only do we profess belief in a church that is both holy and catholic, but also in one that is apostolic:

> The apostles are dead; there are no new apostles. But the *apostolic mission* remains. The mission of the apostles was more than the persons of the apostles themselves . . . *Who* then are the followers of the apostles?. . . There can only be one basic answer: the Church. The whole Church, not just a few individuals, is the follower of the apostles.[14]

Yes, "We believe in one holy catholic and apostolic Church." As such, we believe in a church that is holy because it is given to us through the power of the Holy Spirit, which is of God. As holy, the church is set apart to be *in* the world, but not *of* the world.

In addition, we believe in a church that is catholic, or universal — for everyone, everywhere, from all walks of life.

Furthermore, we believe in an apostolic church in which we, as the body of Christ in the world, are meant to carry on the mission of the apostles.

What responsibility do these words carry for our mission and ministry in the world today?

CONCLUSION

A number of individuals who read this manuscript have not only urged but pleaded with me to write a conclusion. "What am I to do now that I have read this?" they ask. "I can no longer repeat the Nicene Creed in church without thinking about what you have written."

If that is the immediate result of reading this book, then my initial purpose has been accomplished. As stated in the Preface, it has been my desire to uncover and recover part of the Christian tradition that has been lost. The uncovering may be joyful for some, and painful for others, while raising a host of questions for all. Just as my original research for *Recovering Lost Tradition* raised a number of questions for me, so too has my research for this book.

For example, given the material presented in chapter II regarding the designation of God as Father in the Nicene Creed, is it still appropriate to hold up only this one image of God in the creed? Is the use of this one image faithful to the richness and complexity of the Christian tradition? Throughout this book, I have demonstrated that it is not. The time has come for the church as an ecumenical body to discuss the images of God used in the central statement of our faith. Is it not now time for another ecumenical council?

In raising this question, I am aware that most books written on the subject of God-language and trinitarian language are written at the academic level. Very few lay people have been exposed to the teaching that occurs daily in seminaries regarding current biblical scholarship and theology on this issue. Thus, for the issue to be appropriately addressed, more books need to be written and more dialogue needs to occur that is accessible to academics, clergy, and laity alike. My book is intended as a further contribution toward that end.

With regard to the issues I have raised regarding the Trinity as eternally and essentially beyond gender designation, I feel strongly that such teaching needs to occur in today's church. The time is past when only one strand of Christian tradition — the patriarchal strand — can be taught. Why would any of us want to continue to hold up only part of the tradition of our church?

As the apostolic church, I believe our mission is to reach out, to evaluate, and where possible, to include the insights of diverse theologians of all ethnic backgrounds throughout the Christian communion — not just the first-world church, not predominantly males, but everyone. To weave a rich tapestry we need many different threads. We need courage for people to speak out. We need patience with one another as we undergo this process and above all, we need love.

I have written in the section on the Trinity that God's fundamental self-revelation is love. It is through God's love for us that we are able to love others in return.

May we have enough love and respect for the tradition of our church not to highlight parts of the tradition while excluding others. May we have enough love and respect for one another not to listen to some to the exclusion of others. May we have enough love for the truth not to run away from it when we hear it.

Yes, we believe in one God, in one Lord Jesus Christ, and in the Holy Spirit. Let us never forget this as we, as an ecumenical body, discuss these and other issues so central to our faith and mission in the world today.

STUDY GUIDE

Session 1
(Chapter I)

1. Have participants reflect on the first article of the Nicene Creed, "We believe in one God, the Father, the Almighty, maker of heaven and earth, of all that is seen and unseen." Then ask them to state what they mean when they recite the words "We believe in one God."

2. Read aloud the story from *Entertaining Angels*, Handout IA. Then ask, "Have you ever had an encounter with someone of another faith? What was that like for you?"

3. Recount the story of the beginnings of Judaism, Christianity, and Islam as related in Chapter I. Discuss how the first five words of the Creed include all three faiths.

4. Write the following quote from Renita Weems on newsprint. Ask for responses to it.

> As black and white women in America, as Israeli and Lebanese women, as white South African and black South African women, as Asian and European women . . . working for righteousness in splendid isolation from one another is a luxury we cannot afford.
>
> Renita J. Weems, *Just a Sister Away* (San Diego: Lura Media, 1988), 18.

5. Write "We believe in one God" on newsprint and ask participants what this phrase means to them now.

Henry Ralph Carse, a Christian living in Israel, relates an incident in which he is welcomed hospitably by strangers on a Christmas eve in Bethlehem, just after the Six Day War.

On Christmas Eve, I walked to Bethlehem, naively expecting to attend the Midnight Mass. From Jerusalem to the very threshold of the Basilica of the Nativity, the roads were crowded with the limousines of ecclesiastical and otherwise distinguished personalities. At the church, all the entrances were heavily guarded by Israeli security forces; only visitors armed with special passes could gain entrance.

It was nearly midnight. Once I had left the crush of activity in Manger Square I found the narrow streets of Bethlehem very quiet. I wandered aimlessly, beginning to feel thoroughly chilled, wondering in my innocence if I would find a youth hostel. Instead, I passed a narrow lighted doorway, and turned to enter it, hearing a cheerful levantine "Welcome!" from within. It was a tiny barber shop of sorts, and there indeed was the elderly proprietor giving a young man what I suppose was a well-lathered Turkish shave. Immediately I was made to feel at ease, offered a low stool and showered with curious questions. The shave was abandoned, three cups of very hot sweet tea were produced from the shadows, and our rough conversation turned, naturally enough, to religion.

My hosts were, they informed me, Moslems, but not, of course, they assured me hurriedly, the kind who don't shave. Not feeling particularly enlightened by this disclosure, I asked them how they felt about the big birthday celebrations which had turned their home town into an international V.I.P. event. They laughed, and the younger man said, "This is nothing. You heard how Prophet Mohammed born?" Of course I hadn't.

In the stillest, smallest hours of Christmas Day, in a Bethlehem barber shop, I listened in fascination to the miraculous birth tale of Allah's messenger. The two men shared in the telling, vying to improve each other's English delivery, drawn by my listening into a strange excitement, reaching for half-remembered details which would give the story oriental perfection. Their voices, their faces, reflected not only pride and confidence, but something like relief; it was exactly as if they had been waiting a long time for someone who had never heard . . . . [8]

Elizabeth Geitz, *Entertaining Angels* (Harrisburg, PA: Morehouse Publishing, 1993), 37-38. Reprinted with permission.

Session 2
(Chapters II and III)

1. Brainstorm with the group and list all the names for God the group can think of. Write them on newsprint.

2. Give out Handout 2A and have one participant after another read one of the scripture passages aloud. At the conclusion, ask for their reactions to the reading.

3. Relate the experience of the author when she began praying with different images of God, found on page 21. Share the poem "Gentle Guide," Handout 2B, and have someone read it aloud. Ask how they think their prayer life might be affected if they prayed with a different image of God.

4. If time permits, engage the group in a dramatic role play to discover the nature of the God to whom we pray. It should help participants articulate their images of God and focus on how people in different contexts might visualize God. Give out Handouts 2C and 2D for this exercise. If time is limited, use the Alternative to Role Play exercise. These exercises are from Elizabeth Geitz and Margaret Prescott, *Recovering Lost Tradition,* (Princeton: Trinity Church, 1988), 23-4.

5. Read aloud the male and female images for God used throughout the history of Christianity, found in Chapters II and III.

6. Give out the following quote by Tilden Edwards. Have one person read it aloud, then ask the group for their response.

> The names of God in scripture reflect all kinds of images . . . Perhaps each of us images God in all of the ways at some time or another. At any given time, though, we likely relate more to some of these than others. Because they all express some dimension of that Ultimate Reality whose Presence we sense, it is important that a person sense their ultimate alignment. Even though one dimension may have more value at a given point, the others correct and fill out the image. One alone can become distorting and destructive.
>
> Tilden Edwards, *Spiritual Friend* (New York: Paulist Press, 1980), 139.

6. Write "We believe in one God, the Father, the Almighty, maker of heaven and earth" on newsprint. Ask participants what this phrase means to them now.

Handout 2A

IMAGES OF GOD FROM SCRIPTURE

Genesis 18:25 [Abraham is talking to God.] "Far be it from you to do such a thing, to slay the righteous with the wicked, so that the righteous fare as the wicked! Far be that from you! Shall not the **Judge** of all the earth do what is just?"

Exodus 3:14 God said to Moses, "I AM WHO I AM." He said further, "Thus you shall say to the Israelites, 'I AM has sent me to you.'"

Deuteronomy 31:30, 32:18 Then Moses recited the words of this song, to the very end, in the hearing of the whole assembly of Israel: "You are unmindful of the **Rock** who bore you; you forgot the **God who gave you birth.**"

2 Samuel 22:3 My God, my **rock,** in whom I take refuge, my **shield** and the horn of my salvation.

Job 38:3, 29 [God asks Job.] "Who shut in the sea with doors when it burst out from the **womb?**" "From whose womb did the ice come forth, and **who has given birth** to the hoarfrost of heaven?"

Isaiah 42:14 [God is speaking to the Israelites.] "For a long time I have held my peace, I have kept still and restrained myself; now I will cry out like **a woman in labor,** I will gasp and pant."

Isaiah 66:12, 13 For thus says the LORD: . . . "As a **mother** comforts her child, so I will comfort you."

Hosea 13:7-8 [God is speaking to the Israelites.] "I will become like a **lion** to them, like a **leopard** I will lurk beside the way. I will fall upon them like a **bear robbed of her cubs.**"

Hosea 14:5 [God is speaking to the Israelites.] "I will be like the **dew** to Israel; he shall blossom like the lily."

Mark 14:36 He [Jesus] said, **"Abba, Father,** for you all things are possible."

Luke 15:4 [Jesus told these parables about the nature of God.], "Which one of you, having a hundred sheep and losing one of them, does not leave the ninety-nine in the wilderness and go after the one that is lost until he finds it?" **(shepherd searching for a lost sheep)**

Luke 15:8 "Or what woman having ten silver coins, if she loses one of them, does not light a lamp, sweep the house, and search carefully until she finds it?" **(woman searching for a lost coin)**

Luke 15:11 Then Jesus said, "There was a man who had two sons . . . the younger son gathered all he had and traveled to a distant country, and there he squandered his property in dissolute living . . . But while he was still far off, his father saw him and was filled with compassion. **(compassionate father)**

Hebrews 12:29 "For indeed our God is a **consuming fire.**"

GENTLE GUIDE

O God of many names, God beyond my naming,
Images swirl through my head.
Which ones for me now? Which one will work,
Since 'Father' is but one among many?

O Great Patriarch, King of all creation,
Your little girl's not little anymore.
Images are shed before others fill the void
Leaving me vulnerable, raw, and exposed.

How to relate, how to commune
With this new-found, Transcendent Other,
Eluding my grasp, escaping my reach,
Moving like mist through my fingers?

Don't try to force it, just let it come,
Through the Source from which you draw strength.
Breathe in, breathe out, relax, be at peace
And trust in your God, your Creator.

"You've sent me a bird? An animal? That's strange!
What am I to do now?"
"Climb up, nestle in, there's a place for you here,
In the down that is under my wing."

Safe and secure, upward we soar,
The sound of the wind rushing by.
Gliding, sailing, new destinies await,
This explorer and her gentle Guide.

—Elizabeth Rankin Geitz

ROLE PLAY SITUATIONS

GOD ROLES:

ROLE #1 God as Judge

ROLE #2 God as Father

ROLE #3 God as Mother

ROLE #4 God as Shield, Fortress, Rock

ROLE #5 God as the Almighty, Holy One

HUMAN ROLES:

ROLE #6 You are middle-aged and have just lost your job. You have a family and a mortgage. You would like to change careers but are afraid to do so.

ROLE #7 You are going through a divorce. It is a painful, angry process. You are fighting over custody of the children and the financial settlement.

ROLE #8 You are a child in an abusive family. Your father has abused you. Your mother seems unable to admit this and protect you. You don't know where to turn and are filled with self-blame.

ROLE #9 You are a pregnant, unwed teenage girl. Your family has rejected you and your boyfriend refuses responsibility. You are staying with a friend's family. What should you do?

ROLE #10 You have been accused of drunk driving. You

hit another car and the other driver was killed. You are brought to trial for homicide by auto.

ROLE #11 You are very ill with a life-threatening disease. You have a young family still dependent on you. They are devastated by your illness. You are afraid for them and for yourself.

ROLE #12 You are a single parent in the inner-city. You have just lost your home due to rising rents fueled by gentrification. Your children were taken away from you as you can no longer provide shelter for them.

INSTRUCTIONS FOR ROLE PLAY

1. RELAX. This does not require an Actor's Equity card! Think of it as a rehearsal rather than as a performance. The purpose is to begin to articulate our images of God and to get an idea of how people in different contexts might view God. Read the description of your role. As you focus on these roles use your own images that arise when you use these names for God. Get in touch with your internalized pictures of God. Consider the scripture passages we just read for further insights into God seen as Father, Mother, Judge, etc.

If you have a "human" role to play, decide which image of God you would approach. Be prepared to have a brief conversation with God about your situation. Describe what happened and how you feel. Decide if you want to make any request of God.

If you have been given a "God" role, think what this image of God might be like. Then read the human roles and decide how you would respond if approached by any of these people. What would you say or do as this image of God? Be prepared to respond verbally and/or physically to any of these people. Take about 10 minutes to get into your role.

2. **Human Roles:** Briefly act out your encounter with the God image of your choice. Describe your situation and needs to God.

3. **God Roles:** Respond verbally and/or physically to each human situation presented to you.

Take no more than 30 minutes for your "drama."

Session 3
(Chapter IV)

1. Read the second article of the Nicene Creed aloud. Ask participants to reflect on what they mean when they recite these words of the creed.

2. Have participants complete the exercise "Guess the Century," on Handout 3A. After they are finished, discuss the answers found on Handout 3B.

3. Present the material in Chapter IV in lecture format, stressing the significance of Jesus' humanity versus his maleness. Relate this to the references to Jesus as mother throughout the centuries.

5. Read aloud the following quotation, then ask, "What might it do to your self-image to never see yourself in the likeness of Christ? How might the world be different if both women and men could be seen in Christ's image?"

> Theological assertions that the risen Christ transcends the concrete particulars of history do not have the power that a single image has to bring about this emotional healing and focus for worship. Women's imaginations need the deep emotional healing and affirmation that come from seeing the image and likeness of Christ conveyed more fully in relation to them . . . To say that Christ cannot be imaged as a woman is to imply that women cannot, in fact, image Christ.
>
> Kathleen Fischer, *Women at the Well* (New York: Paulist Press, 1988), 81.

GUESS THE CENTURY

Match the date and name on the second page with the quotation on this page.

_____ 1. Word spoken by God, light, life, wisdom, power: all these names are yours, and I use them all to greet you with. Fruit, invention, image of the great Mind; as word spiritual, as human visible; firmly uttered by God to be the support of all things and to bind them together . . .

_____ 2. The Word (Christ) is everything to His little ones, both father and mother . . .

_____ 3. But you, Jesus, good lord, are you not also a mother? Are you not that mother who, like a hen, collects her chickens under her wings? Truly, master, you are a mother. For what others have conceived and given birth to, they have received from you . . . You are the author, others are the ministers. It is then you, above all, Lord God, who are mother.

_____ 4. As we know, our own mother bore us only into pain and dying. But our true mother Jesus, who is all love, bears us into joy and endless living.

_____ 5. We render thanks to you, O God, through your beloved child Jesus Christ, whom in the last times you sent to us as saviour and redeemer and angel of your will.

_____ 6. For the most part God chooses to relate himself to us as masculine [as the male Jesus].

_____ 7. Honk if you love Jesus.

_____ 8. Let us put our egg under the wings of that Hen of

the Gospel, which crieth out to that false and abandoned city, "O Jerusalem, Jerusalem, how often would I have gathered thy children together, even as a hen her chickens, and thou wouldst not!"

_____ 9. God is now manifesting Himself, and has been for over 450 years, in the form of the Black American woman as mother, as wife, as nourisher, sustainer, and preserver of life, the Suffering Servant who is despised and rejected by men, a personality of sorrow who is acquainted with grief. The Black Woman has borne our griefs and carried our sorrows.

_____ 10. Christ came to me in the likeness of a woman, clad in a bright robe, and he planted wisdom in me.

A. 11th century prayer, Anslem of Canterbury

B. 20th century, Donald Bloesch

C. 4th century Eucharistic liturgy, Apostolic Tradition of Hippolytus

D. 14th century, Julian of Norwich

E. 20th century, William Eichelberger

F. 4th century, St. Augustine

G. 20th century bumper sticker

H. 2nd century, Clement of Alexandria

I. 2nd century, Priscilla

J. 4th century prayer, St. Gregory Nazianzus

Handout 3B

LEADER'S KEY

___J___ 1. Fourth century prayer by St. Gregory Nazianzus, one of the Cappadocian Fathers. He was influential in restoring the Nicene faith and leading to its final establishment at the Council of Constantinople in 381.
(F. Forrester Church, et al., *Earliest Christian Prayers,* New York, Macmillan Publishing Co., 1988, p. 88)

___H___ 2. Written in the second century by Clement of Alexandria, head of the Catechetical School at Alexandria. (Virginia Mollenkott, *The Divine Feminine,* New York, Crossroad, 1983, p. 8)

___A___ 3. Prayer to St. Paul by Anselm of Canterbury, an eleventh century Benedictine monk who became Archbishop of Canterbury in 1093.
(Caroline Walker Bynum, *Jesus as Mother: Studies in the Spirituality of the High Middle Ages,* Berkeley, University of California Press, 1982, p. 114)

___D___ 4. Written in the fourteenth century by Julian of Norwich, an English mystic who wrote *The Sixteen Revelations of Divine Love.*
(Robert Llewelyn, ed., *Enfolded in Love: Daily Readings with Julian of Norwich,* London, Darton, Longman and Todd, 1980, p. 36)

___C___ 5. An excerpt from the Apostolic Tradition of Hippolytus, the first written Eucharist, fourth century. (Jasper and Cuming, eds., *Prayers of the Eucharist: Early and Reformed,* New York, Oxford University Press, 1980, p. 35)

___B___ 6. Written in the twentieth century by Donald Bloesch.
(Donald Bloesch, *The Battle for the Trinity: The Debate over Inclusive God-Language*, Ann Arbor, MI, Servant, 1985, p. 33)

___G___ 7. A twentieth century bumper sticker (an easy question for those having difficulty!)

___F___ 8. Written by St. Augustine of Hippo, a fourth century bishop, whose influence on the development of the theology of the church has been immense. He is known for the full articulation of the doctrine of Original Sin. (Mollenkott, p. 100)

___E___ 9. Written in the twentieth century by William Eichelberger.
("Reflections on the Person and Personality of the Black Messiah," *The Black Church II*, p. 54)

___I___ 10. Written in the second century by Priscilla, a leader in the Montanist movement.

Session 4
(Chapter VI)

1. Write the words "Virgin Mary" on newsprint. Ask the group for descriptive words or phrases that come to mind. Write their answers on newsprint.

2. Discuss Pope Paul VI's portrayal of Mary as the first and most perfect disciple, p. 47 and Deborah Middleton's portrayal of her as co-creator, p. 49. Are these images of Mary different or similar to the phrases used to describe her in the previous exercise?

3. Discuss the depiction of Mary in Christian art, particu-

larly the Icon of Our Lady of the Sign, p. 48. Discuss the illustration on p. 52 which portrays Mary as celebrant at a eucharistic meal. How are these portrayals similar to or different from traditional Christian art depicting Mary?

4. Write the following question on newsprint: "If Mary had not responded affirmatively to the angel Gabriel, how might your life be different today?" Have participants discuss it with one other person in the group, then share with the group as a whole.

5. Discuss Mary's active rather than passive role in the incarnation as described in the original Greek text of the creed, p. 50.

6. Distribute Handout 4A, Hadewijch's *To Learn Mary's Humility*. Have one person read it aloud, then ask the group for their response.

7. Write the phrase "was incarnate of the Holy Spirit *and* the Virgin Mary and became truly *human.*" What does this phrase of the creed mean to you now?

To Learn Mary's Humility

The mystical reflections of Hadewijch written in the 13th century, set the mystery of Mary's life in the context which best celebrates her role and ours as those who long to bear God's life to others.

David said that when he remembered
    God, he was moved
And his spirit swooned away.
    He indeed was called strong in work,
    But Mary wrought a work of greater strength.
Truly David bore the largest share of that great work
Save for Mary, who received him totally.
As God and as Infant.
There can we first perceive
The genuine work of Love.

It was by deep longing
That this mystery happened to her,
That this noble Love was released
    To this noble woman
    Of high praise
In overflowing measure,

Because she wished nothing else and owned nothing else,
She wholly possessed him of whom every Jewish woman
had read.

Session 5
(Chapter VII)

1. Begin by having the group sing together, "Were You There When They Crucified My Lord?"

2. Discuss who was there when they crucified our Lord and who was not, p. 53. Ask why this might have been the case.

3. Give out Dorothy Sayer's quote from *Are Women Human?* found on pages 53 and 54. Have participants read aloud one phrase of the quote, then have the next person read a phrase, etc. Have them discuss their reactions in pairs and then with the group as a whole.

4. Present another possible reason why the women stayed at the foot of the cross from the perspective of Black women and women in developing nations, pages 54-55. Elicit responses from the group.

5. Give out Handout 5A, "Easter Mourning," and have someone read the poem aloud. Have participants discuss with one other person a time in their own lives when they have felt forsaken by God. Discuss the last stanza as a group, discussing how they might give birth to the One that dwells within them.

6. Discuss the concept of Christ giving birth to the church on the cross in light of page 55. Show the detail from the French Moralized Bible, p. 60. Discuss.

7. End by singing again, "Were You There When They Crucified My Lord?"

EASTER MOURNING

The smell of lilies permeates my senses
As alleluias ring through the air.
"Rejoice. Christ is risen. Yes, risen indeed!"
Yet for me, I'm still on Golgotha.

Weeping, kneeling at the foot of the cross
Wounds bleeding, water flowing to mesh with my tears.
Ashes to ashes, dust to dust
But not now, not here, not this way!

"My God, my God, why have you forsaken me?"
O Wounded One, don't leave me, not now.
My pain is your pain and your pain is mine.
Flesh rips, hearts bleed, then it stops.

Now I'll carry you, as you've carried me
Giving birth to the you now within me.
Hearts mingle, tears spill as my love overflows
For the Wounded One, Risen One, life-giving Lover of Souls.

—Elizabeth Rankin Geitz

Session 6
(Chapter VIII)

1. Have participants reflect on the following portion of
the creed, "On the third day he rose again in accordance
with the scriptures; he ascended into heaven and is seated
at the right hand of the Father." Then ask them to say what
it means to them that Jesus rose from the dead.

2. Write the words "Mary Magdalene" on newsprint. Ask the group for descriptive words or phrases that come to mind. Write them on newsprint.

3. If possible, xerox on a transparency *Mary Magdalene Proclaims the Resurrection to the Disciples,* found on the cover of this book. Project it onto a screen with an overhead projector. Discuss Mary Magdalene as the "apostle to the apostles," as related on pages 64-65.

4. Have participants gather in groups of three and discuss the following questions: "Have you, like Mary, ever been disbelieved when you tried to relate an important event in your life? What was that like for you? How do you imagine Mary Magdalene felt?"

5. Discuss the status of women in Jesus' day. Then discuss how Jesus related to women throughout his ministry. See pages 61-62.

6. Write the following quotation on newsprint. Have participants discuss it in small groups, then with the group as a whole in light of the significance it has for women and men today:

> The evangelists' description of Jesus' "first appearing to and commissioning of women to bear witness to the most important event of his career cannot be understood as anything but deliberate; it was a dramatic linking of a very clear rejection of the second-class status of women with the center of Jesus' gospel, his resurrection."
>
> Leonard Swidler, *Biblical Affirmations of Woman* (Philadelphia: Westminster Press, 1979), 204-5.

7. End by singing "You Shall Be My Witnesses," Handout 6A, words and music by Miriam Therese Winter.

You Shall Be My Witnesses

Refrain

You shall be my wit-ness-es through all the earth,
tell-ing of all you have heard and re-ceived, for I a-rose and am
with you and you have be-lieved.

Fine **Verses**

Wom-en at the tomb,
Mag-da-lene at the tomb:
Wom-en, leave your tombs.

weep-ing for the dead: He is not here, he has ri-sen as he
Whom do you seek? Her eyes were o-pened when she heard him
Roll the stones a-side. Do not des-pair, though so man-y dreams have

said. They ran to tell those who were in au-thor-i-
speak. His love for ev'-ry wom-an shone up-on his
died. Do not be fear-ful of the vi-sion that you

ty. The men dis-missed the news as i-dle fan-ta-sy.
face. The hopes of ev'-ry age were held in their em-brace.
see. Be-lieve in mir-a-cles a-gain. Be-lieve in me.

Words and music by Miriam Therese Winter
© Medical Mission Sisters 1987

Session 7
(Chapter IX)

1. Begin by playing the audio tape of *Veni Sancte Spiritus,* which means Come Holy Spirit, found on the Taizé tape, *Cantate,* music by Jacques Berthier.

2. On newsprint write, "We believe in the Holy Spirit, the Lord, the giver of life." Have participants reflect on what these words mean to them. Write their reflections on newsprint.

3. Read aloud the Thanksgiving over the Water from the baptismal service in *The Book of Common Prayer,* p. 306-7. (Denominations other than Episcopalian should read from their baptismal service, focusing on the section related to the Holy Spirit.) What is the connection between the Holy Spirit and birth?

4. Read aloud John 3:4-5. What is the connection between the Holy Spirit and our second birth?

5. Discuss Elizabeth Johnson's theory about the neglect of the Holy Spirit in theological discourse as discussed on pages 70-71.

6. Give out the following quote from Karen Bloomquist:

> Patriarchy ... arose as a compensation for men's physiological inability to give birth. In early societies, giving birth connoted a divine power, especially when the male role in procreation was not yet known. Females, in being able to reproduce themselves, exhibited greater permanence and were experienced as having the key to immortality in a way that males did not.
>
> Karen Bloomquist, "Let God Be God," *Our Naming of God: Problems and Prospects of God-Talk Today* (Minneapolis, MN: Fortress Press, 1989), 52.

Thus, to achieve a position of power, the male was moved to dominate the woman's sexuality and reproductive capacity in a way that the female became the private property of the male, thus giving rise to the patriarchal system. Does this seem plausible to you? Why or why not?

7. Discuss the significance of the Holy Spirit as "Lord" as found on pages 72-74.

8. Write, "We believe in the Holy Spirit, the Lord, the giver of life." What does the beginning of the third article of the creed mean to you now?

Session 8
(Chapter IX on the Trinity)

1. Draw a triangle on newsprint, writing "Father, Son and Holy Spirit," in the three points. Ask participants to reflect on what this means to them in terms of their relationship with God.

2. Discuss the current debate regarding the Trinity as related on pages 77-81. Since this material is rather complicated, participants should read the material ahead of time.

3. Stress that if the three persons are of one substance, or *ousia,* and the one substance is without body, as the first of the Thirty-Nine Articles states, then all three persons of the Trinity must of necessity be eternally and essentially beyond gender distinctions. Asserting that any of the three persons is essentially and eternally gender-bound is theologically inaccurate and against the underlying theology of the Nicene Creed.

4. Write on newsprint the following quotation from E. J. Bicknell:

All theologians confess that the best [Trinitarian] language that can be found is inadequate. The Church only uses these words, because she cannot escape . . . The [church] Fathers are full of similar confessions of the inadequacy of human language.

Bicknell, *A Theological Introduction to the Thirty-Nine Articles of the Church of England* (London: Longmans, Green and Co, 1919) p. 50.

Discuss as a group.

5. Draw a triangle on newsprint and write the words "Lover, Beloved, and the Love that Exists Between Them." Explain in light of St. Augustine, pages 82-84. Would expanding Trinitarian language to reflect this part of our tradition be desirable? Why or why not?

6. Ask participants how they feel now when reciting the Nicene Creed in church. Relate some of the material from the Conclusion. Is there a next step? Why or why not? If yes, what might it be and how might they participate?

NOTES

Preface
1. Eduard Schweizer, Class handout, Princeton Theological Seminary.

2. The term *womanist* was first coined by Alice Walker. She defines a womanist as "a black feminist or feminist of color . . . committed to survival and wholeness of entire people, male *and* female." *In Search of our Mothers' Gardens* (San Diego, CA: Harcourt Brace Jovanovich, 1983), xi.

3. Evelyn Underhill, *The School of Charity: Meditations on the Christian Creed* (Harrisburg, PA: Morehouse Publishing, 1991), xiii.

Chapter I
1. Gerald O'Collins, S.J. and Mary Venturini, *Believing: Understanding the Creed* (New York: Paulist Press, 1991), 25.

2. Trevor Huddleston, *I Believe: Reflections on the Creed* (London: Fount Paperbacks, 1986), 13.

3. Renita J. Weems, *Just a Sister Away: A Womanist Vision of Women's Relationships in the Bible* (San Diego, CA: Luramedia, 1988), 1. Even though black women see their story in the story of Hagar, Weems asserts whereas ancient people were indeed aware of one another's color,

"there is no evidence that race and color, as we understand them today, especially as a way of stratifying people, prevailed at that time" (p. 1). She points out that the differences between the two women were centered more in their contrasting economic positions (p. 3).

4. Ibid., 18.

5. Carl E. Braaten, ed., *Our Naming of God: Problems and Prospects of God-Talk Today* (Minneapolis, MN: Fortress Press, 1989), 66.

Chapter II
1. St. Cyril of Jerusalem, *The Catechetical Lectures of St. Cyril of Jerusalem* (Oxford: J.H. Parker, 1838), 152.

2. Carl E. Braaten, ed., *Our Naming of God: Problems and Prospects of God-Talk Today* (Minneapolis, MN: Fortress Press, 1989), 62.

3. Elizabeth Geitz and Margaret Prescott, *Recovering Lost Tradition* (Princeton, NJ: Trinity Church, 1988), 19-20.

4. Ibid.

5. St. Clement of Alexandria, *Paedagogus, The Ante-Nicene Fathers: The Writings of the Fathers down to A.D. 325,* ed. Alexander Roberts and James Donaldson, vol. 2 (New York: Charles Scribner's Sons, 1908), 220-221, quoted in Jann Aldredge Clanton, *In Whose Image? God and Gender* (New York: Crossroad, 1990), 40.

6. St. Ambrose, *The Sacrament of the Incarnation of Our Lord, Theological and Dogmatic Works*, trans. Roy J. Defarrari (Washington: The Catholic University of America Press, 1963), 223, quoted in Clanton's *In Whose Image*, 41.

7. Luther, *Lectures on Isaiah, Chapters 40-66*, ed. Hilton

C. Oswald, *Luther's Works*, Vol. 17 (St. Louis, MO: Concordia, 1972); 139.

8. Calvin, *Commentary on the Book of the Prophet Isaiah*, trans. William Pringle, vol. 4 (Edinburgh: Calvin Translation Society, 1858), 30.

9. St. Gertrude of Helfta, *Legatus*, Book 5, ch. 8, p. 54, and Book 4, ch. 5, p. 314. Quoted in Caroline Walker Bynum, *Jesus as Mother* (Berkeley: Univ. of California Press, 1982), 190.

10. Rowan Williams, *Resurrection: Interpreting the Easter Gospel* (Harrisburg, PA: Morehouse Publishing, 1994), 71,73.

11. Elizabeth A. Johnson, *She Who Is: The Mystery of God in Feminist Theological Discourse* (New York: Crossroad, 1993), 80.

12. Tilden H. Edwards, *Spiritual Friend: Reclaiming the Gift of Spiritual Direction* (New York: Paulist Press, 1980), 138-39. Italics added.

13. John R. Kohlenberger III, ed., *The NRSV Concordance Unabridged* (Grand Rapids, MI: Harper Collins, 1991), 444-45.

14. James Dunn, *Christology in the Making* (Philadelphia: Westminster Press, 1980), 30, quoted in Johnson *She Who Is*.

15. St. Cyril of Jerusalem, *Catechetical Lectures*, 160.

16. Johnson, *She Who Is*, 35.

17. St. Thomas Aquinas, *Summa Theologiae*, First Part, Question 119, Article 2.

18. J. Robert Wright, *Readings for the Daily Office from the Early Church* (New York: Church Hymnal Corporation, 1991), 132.

19. *The Book of Common Prayer*, (New York: The Church Hymnal Corp., 1979), 867.

20. Alice Walker, *The Color Purple* (New York: Washington Square Press, 1983) quoted in Rachel Hosmer *Gender and God: Love and Desire in Christian Spirituality* (Boston: Cowley Publications, 1986), 119.

21. Johnson, *She Who Is*, 33.

22. Sandra Schneiders, *Women and the Word: The Gender of God in the New Testament and the Spirituality of Women* (New York: Paulist Press, 1986), 17.

23. Kathleen Fischer, *Women at the Well: Feminist Perspectives on Spiritual Direction* (New York: Paulist Press, 1988), 60.

24. Sallie McFague, *Metaphorical Theology: Models of God in Religious Language* (Philadelphia: Fortress, 1982), 32, 117.

25. St. Thomas Aquinas, *Summa Theologiae*, First Part, Question 13, Article 2.

26. Ibid.

27. Pierre Teilhard de Chardin, *The Divine Milieu: An Essay on the Interior Life* (New York: Harper and Row, 1960), 57.

28. Ibid., 58.

Chapter III
1. Robert Young, ed., *Analytical Concordance to the Bible* (New York: Funk and Wagnalls Co., 1939), 634-35, 69.

2. *Webster's Third New International Dictionary*, ed. Philip B. Gove, (Springfield, MA: G.C. Merriam Co., 1961), 2639.

3. Gerald O'Collins, S.J. and Mary Venturini, *Believing: Understanding the Creed* (New York: Paulist Press, 1991), 43.

4. Virginia Mollenkott, *The Divine Feminine* (New York: Crossroad, 1987), 16.

Chapter IV
1. Karl Barth, *Credo* (London: Hodder and Stoughton, 1935), 45.

2. Ibid., 46.

3. Rosemary Radford Ruether, *To Change the World: Christology and Cultural Criticism* (New York: Crossroad, 1986), 45.

4. Donald Bloesch, *The Battle for the Trinity: The Debate over Inclusive-God Language* (Ann Arbor, MI: Servant, 1985) 33.

5. Thomas F. Torrance, "The Christian Apprehension of God the Father," in *Speaking the Christian God: The Holy Trinity and the Challenge of Feminism*, ed. Alvin F. Kimel Jr. (Grand Rapids, MI: William B. Eerdman's Publishing Co., 1992) 135-36.

6. Patricia Wilson-Kastner, *Faith, Feminism, and the Christ* (Philadelphia: Fortress Press, 1983), 90.

7. Jacquelyn Grant, "Womanist Theology: Black Women's Experience," in *Black Theology: A Documentary History*, vol. II, ed. James H. Cone and Gayraud S. Wilmore, (New York: Orbis Books, 1993), 53.

8. St. Athanasius, *On the Incarnation* (Crestwood, NY: St. Vladimir's Seminary Press, 1989), 29.

9. Ibid.

10. J. Robert Wright, *Readings for the Daily Office from the Early Church* (New York: The Church Hymnal Corp., 1991), 42.

11. Ibid., 38.

12. Virginia Mollenkott, *The Divine Feminine* (New York: Crossroad, 1983), 93-94.

13. Ibid., 100.

14. Caroline Walker Bynum, *Jesus as Mother: Studies in the Spirituality of the High Middle Ages* (Berkeley: Univ. of California Press, 1982), 114.

15. The Standing Liturgical Commission of the Episcopal Church, *Supplemental Liturgical Texts: Prayer-Book Studies 30* (New York: The Church Hymnal Corporation, 1989), 72.

16. The Standing Liturgical Commission of the Episcopal Church, *Supplemental Liturgical Materials*, (New York: The Church Hymnal Corporation, 1991), 40.

17. Barth, *Credo*, 46.

18. St. Athanasius, *On the Incarnation*, 26. Italics added.

19. Robert W. Bertram, "Putting the Nature of God into Language: Naming the Trinity" in *Our Naming of God: Problems and Prospects of God-Talk Today* (Minneapolis, MN: Fortress Press, 1989), 108.

20. Sarah Coakley, "Presentation of Women's Reflections

of the Lambeth Conference" (England: Christian Communication Co., 1988), Videotape.

21. Marianne H. Micks, *Loving the Questions: An Exploration of the Nicene Creed* (Boston: Cowley Publications, 1993), 51.

22. Mary Tanner, "Presentation of Women's Reflections of the Lambeth Conference" (England: Christian Communication Co., 1988), videotape.

23. Mollenkott, *The Divine Feminine*, 8.

24. Ibid., 9.

25. Ibid., 22.

26. St. Augustine, *The Confessions, The City of God, On Christian Doctrine* (Chicago: Britannica, 1952), 50.

27. Bynum, *Jesus as Mother*, 117.

28. St. Catherine of Siena, Letter to Urban VI. Quoted in Katharina M. Wilson, ed., *Medieval Women Writers* (Georgia: Univ. of Georgia Press, 1984), 257.

29. Robert Llewelyn, ed., *Enfolded in Love: Daily Readings with Julian of Norwich* (London: Darton, Longman, and Todd, 1980), 36.

30. St. Julian of Norwich, *Showings* (New York: Paulist Press, 1978), 301-2.

31. William Eichelberger, "Reflections on the Person and Personality of the Black Messiah," in *The Black Church II*, 54.

32. St. Hildegard of Bingen in *The Writings of Medieval Women*, Marcelle Thiebaux, transl. (New York: Garland Publishing Co., 1987) 133, 143-144. Quoted in Barbara

Bowe, et al., *Silent Voices, Sacred Lives: Women's Readings for the Liturgical Year* (New York: Paulist Press, 1992), 52-53.

33. Kathleen Fischer, *Women at the Well: Feminist Perspectives on Spiritual Direction* (New York: Paulist 1988), 81.

Chapter V
1. H.C. Kee et al., *Christianity: A Social and Cultural History* (New York: Macmillan Publishing Co., 1991), 139-140.

2. Richard A. Norris, Jr., transl. and ed., *The Christological Controversy* (Philadelphia: Fortress Press, 1980), 17-18.

3. Ibid., 19.

4. Ibid., 18.

5. Frances Young, *The Making of the Creeds* (Philadelphia: Trinity Press International, 1991), 47.

6. Gerald O'Collins, S.J. and Mary Venturini, *Believing: Understanding the Creed* (New York: Paulist Press, 1991), 50.

7. R.C.D. Jasper and G.J. Cuming, eds., *Prayers of the Eucharist: Early and Reformed* (New York: Oxford University Press, 1980) 23.

8. Ibid., 24.

Chapter VI
1. Regarding the depiction of Mary in classical art, womanist theologian Cain Hope Felder writes: "Throughout the world it has become standard for Christians to think of almost all biblical characters from Noah, Abraham,

Miriam, Moses, the pharaohs, even the Queen of Sheba, to Mary and Joseph, and virtually all of the New Testament personalities as typical Europeans. For example . . . pictorial representations of her [Mary] today are invariably the image of a European. This centerpiece of much modern Christian art is perceived as an accurate image of the original Madonna. Consequently, most people believe that the mother of Jesus of Nazareth was a woman who resembled the ordinary European of today. Such presumptions are only now beginning to be substantively challenged by Afrocentric modes of biblical interpretation as studies devote more attention to ancient iconography and the importance of Egyptian and Ethiopian civilizations in the shaping of the biblical world." "Cultural Ideology, Afrocentrism and Biblical Interpretation", in *Black Theology: A Documentary History*, vol. II 1980-1992, ed. James Cone and Gayraud Wilmore (New York: Orbis Books, 1993), 188. It should be noted that not all womanist theologians agree with Felder's viewpoint.

2. Renita J. Weems, *Just A Sister Away: A Womanist Vision of Women's Relationships in the Bible* (San Diego, CA: LuraMedia, 1988), 122.

3. Quoted in Raymond Brown, *The Birth of the Messiah: A Commentary on the Infancy Narratives in Matthew and Luke* (New York: Doubleday, 1977), 259.

4. Deborah F. Middleton, "The Story of Mary: Luke's Version," *New Blackfriars* (1989), 561.

5. J. Robert Wright, Patristics Handout, General Theological Seminary.

6. Ibid.

7. Ibid.

8. Middleton, "The Story of Mary," 561.

9. Standing Liturgical Commission, *Supplemental Liturgical Materials* (New York: The Church Hymnal Corporation, 1991), 52.

10. Wright, Patristics Handout, General Theological Seminary.

11. Richard A. Norris, Jr., "The Beginnings of Christian Priesthood," *Anglican Theological Review* (1984), 30.

Chapter VII
1. Dorothy L. Sayers, *Are Women Human?* (Grand Rapids, MI: William B. Eerdmans Publishing Co., 1971), 47.

2. Jacquelyn Grant, "Womanist Theology: Black Women's Experience," in *Black Theology: Documentary History,* vol. II, ed. James Cone and Gayraud Wilmore, (New York: Orbis Books, 1993), 281.

3. Ibid.

4. Virginia Fabella, "A Christology for Asian Women?" *Daughters of Sarah* 17 (1991), 13.

Chapter VIII
1. Christina Baxter, Dean of St. John's College, Nottingham, England, 1990 Lecture, Princeton Theological Seminary.

2. Leonard Swidler, *Biblical Affirmations of Woman* (Philadelphia: Westminster Press, 1979), 180.

3. Ibid., 180-195.

4. Ibid., 173-74.

5. Ibid., 193.

6. Origen, *Selecta in Exodus* XVIII, 17, Migne, *Patrologia*

Graeca, 12, Cols. 296 f. Quoted in Swidler, *Biblical Affirmations of Woman*, 342.

7. Gerald O'Collins, *Jesus Risen: An Historical Fundamental and Systematic Examination of Christ's Resurrection* (New York: Paulist Press, 1987), 10.

8. Swidler, *Biblical Affirmations of Woman*, 209.

9. Jean Campbell, OSH, "Lectionary Omissions," *The Witness*, 76:5, (May 1993), 22. A longer version of the article is available in *Ruach*, 13:2, 1992, P.O. Box 348, Towaco, NJ 07082.

10. Sally M. Bucklee, "Oh, to be in England, Now That Ordination's Here," *Ruach*, 15:2, 1994, 8. An icon of Mary Magdalene holding a white egg was commissioned for Grace Cathedral, San Francisco, to commemorate the 1988 election of Barbara Harris as the first female bishop in the Anglican Communion. The icon was presented as a gift to the first women ordained to the priesthood in the Church of England by the Episcopal Women's Caucus, United States.

11. From a conversation with J. Robert Wright, 1994.

12. Swidler, *Biblical Affirmations of Woman*, 204-5.

Chapter IX
1. *The Book of Common Prayer*, 306.

2. Galatians 5:22-23 states, "By contrast, the fruit of the Spirit is love, joy, peace, patience, kindness, generosity, faithfulness, gentleness, and self-control." These gifts or fruits of the spirit are all feminine in gender in the original Greek.

3. Elizabeth A. Johnson, *She Who Is: The Mystery of God*

in Feminist Theological Discourse (New York: Crossroad, 1993), 130-31.

4. Janet Sayers, *Sexual Contradictions: Psychology, Psychoanalysis, and Feminism* (London: Tavistock Publications, 1986), 38.

5. Karen Horney, *Feminine Psychology* (New York: W. W. Norton & Co., 1967), 60. See especially the chapters "The Flight from Womanhood: The Masculinity Complex in Women as Viewed by Men and by Women" and "The Distrust Between the Sexes."

As a psychoanalytic pioneer, Karen Horney (1885-1952) questioned some of Sigmund Freud's formulations of psychosexual development, particularly in relation to women. After coming to the United States in 1932, she became one of the founders of the Association for the Advancement of Psychoanalysis and the American Institute for Psychoanalysis.

6. Karen Bloomquist, "Let God Be God," in *Our Naming of God: Problems and Prospects of God-Talk Today* (Minneapolis, MN: Fortress Press, 1989), 52.

7. For a more in-depth discussion of this concept see Gerda Lerner, *The Creation of Patriarchy* (Oxford: Oxford University Press, 1986)

8. Adrienne Rich, *Of Woman Born: Motherhood as Experience and Institution* (New York: Bantam Books, 1977), 187.

9. Roger Langley and Richard C. Levy, *Wife Beating: The Silent Crisis* (New York, Simon & Schuster, 1977), 103. See also Richard J. Gelles, "Violence and Pregnancy," *Family Coordinator*.

10. Walter Bauer, ed., *Greek-English Lexicon of the New Testament* (Chicago: Univ. of Chicago Press, 1979), 459-60.

11. *Confessing the One Faith: An Ecumenical Explication of the Apostolic Faith as it is Confessed in the Nicene-Constantinopolitan Creed (381)*, Faith and Order Paper No. 153 (Geneva: World Council of Churches Publication, 1991), 74. This document is the result of a widespread, worldwide consensus of the Faith and Order Committee of the World Council of Churches.

12. Frances Young, *The Making of the Creeds* (Philadelphia: Trinity Press International, 1991), 52-53.

13. Ibid., 53.

14. St. Basil, *On the Holy Spirit* (Crestwood, N.Y.: St. Vladimir's Seminary Press, 1980), 46.

15. Ibid., 60, 73.

16. Young, *The Making of the Creeds*, 53.

17. *The Book of Common Prayer*, 868. Italics added.

18. Ibid. Italics added.

19. E.J. Bicknell, *A Theological Introduction to the Thirty-Nine Articles of the Church of England* (London: Longmans, Green and Co., 1919), 27.

20. Elizabeth Achtemeier, "Exchanging God for 'No Gods,'" in *Speaking the Christian God: The Holy Trinity and the Challenge of Feminism*, ed. Alvin F. Kimel (Grand Rapids, MI: William B. Eerdmans Publishing Co., 1992), 5.

21. Alvin Kimel, *A New Language for God? A Critique of Supplemental Liturgical Texts - Prayer Book Studies 30* (Shaker Heights, Ohio: Episcopalians United, 1990), 11-12.

22. Achtemeier, "Exchanging God for 'No Gods,'" 4.

23. Leonard Hodgson, *The Doctrine of the Trinity* (New York: Charles Scribner's Sons, 1944), 22.

24. Bicknell, *A Theological Introduction to the Thirty-Nine Articles of the Church of England*, 49-50.

25. Ibid., 50. Italics added.

26. For a more in-depth discussion of this concept see Colin Gunton and Christopher Schwobel, *Persons, Divine and Human* (Edinburgh: T. and T. Clark, 1991).

27. *Confessing the One Faith*, 74.

28. Tereza Cavalcanti, "If You Come With Me, I Will Go: Women Prophets in the Hebrew Bible," *Daughters of Sarah* 18:3 (1992), 9-14.

29. Hodgson, *The Doctrine of the Trinity*, 175. Italics added.

30. Ibid., 42.

31. Kenneth Cauthen, *Systematic Theology: A Modern Protestant Approach* (Lewiston, N.Y. : The Edwin Mellen Press, 1986), 125.

32. Hodgson, *The Doctrine of the Trinity*, 42.

33. Cauthen, *Systematic Theology*, 119.

34. Catherine Mowry LaCugna, *God For Us: The Trinity and Christian Life* (San Francisco: Harper Collins, 1991), 12.

35. Ibid., 15.

36. Ibid., 270-71.

37. Patricia Wilson-Kastner, *Faith, Feminism, and the Christ* (Philadelphia: Fortress Press, 1983), 127.

38. Ibid.

39. LaCugna, *God For Us*, 273.

40. Ibid.

41. Ibid., 15.

42. Jürgen Moltmann, *The Trinity and the Kingdom: The Doctrine of God* (San Francisco: Harper & Row, 1981), 160.

43. Ibid., 159-60.

44. Cauthen, *Systematic Theology*, 119.

45. Hodgson, *The Doctrine of the Trinity*, 109.

46. Ibid.

47. Catherine LaCugna, "The Baptismal Formula, Feminist Objections, and Trinitarian Theology," *Journal of Ecumenical Studies* 26 (1989), 235.

48. *Journal of the General Convention of the Episcopal Church 1991* (New York: Episcopal Church Center, 1991), 400.

49. Ruth C. Duck, *Gender and the Name of God: The Trinitarian Baptismal Formula* (New York: The Pilgrim Press, 1991), 163.

50. LaCugna, "The Baptismal Formula," 244.

51. Ibid.

52. Cauthen, *Systematic Theology*, 119.

53. St. Augustine, *The Trinity*, Stephen McKenna, transl. (Washington, DC: Catholic University Press, 1963), 491-2.

Book 15, Chapter 17, Section 27.

54. Ibid., Book 8, Chapter 10, Section 14, p. 266.

55. Quoted in St. Thomas Aquinas, *Summa Theologiae*, First Part, Question 37, Article I.

56. Ibid.

57. Thomas and Hazel Clark, eds., *Christ in Poetry* (New York: Association Press, 1952),125.

58. Wilson-Kastner, *Faith, Feminism, and the Christ*, 89.

59. Evelyn Underhill, *The School of Charity: Meditations on the Christian Creed* (Harrisburg, PA: Morehouse Publishing, 1991), xiii.

Chapter X
1. Karl Barth, *Credo* (London: Hodder and Stoughton, 1935), 127.

2. Trevor Huddleston, *I Believe: Reflections on the Creed* (London: Fount Paperbacks, 1986), 72.

3. Hans Küng, *The Church* (New York: Sheed and Ward, 1967), 130.

4. Ibid. Küng warns against speaking glibly about the church as the people of God. Where does this Christian designation leave Israel and the Jews? He sees a misunderstanding of the Christian church as the people of God, over against the Jews as the people of God, as the root of anti-Semitism: "Did Israel lose its special position as the people of God after the death of Jesus? Not at all, according to Paul; God's faithfulness to Israel persists, even when Israel is unfaithful (Romans 3:3). The vocation of this people of God is continuous, irrevocable, indestructible. The

Jews are and remain God's chosen and beloved people."
For a more in-depth discussion see pp. 132-50.

5. *Confessing the One Faith: An Ecumenical Explication
of the Apostolic Faith as it is Confessed in the Nicene-
Constantinopolitan Creed (381)*, Faith and Order Paper
No. 153 (Geneva: World Council of Churches, 1991), 83.

6. Küng, *The Church*, 130.

7. Ibid., 330.

8. *Confessing the One Faith*, 83.

9. bell hooks, *Ain't I a Woman?* (Boston: South End
Press, 1981), 188.

10. Carter Heyward, Address given at Worldwide Anglican
Encounter in Brazil, quoted in *Ruach* 15:1 (Winter 1994), 18.

11. Rosemary Radford Ruether, "Feminist Theology in
Global Context," *Daughters of Sarah* 17:2 (March/ April
1991), 6.

12. Alice Walker, *Possessing the Secret of Joy* (New York:
Pocket Star Books, 1992), 283.

13. A.M. Rosenthal, "The Torture Continues," *The New
York Times*, July 27,1993, A13.

12. Küng, *The Church*, 130.

PERSON INDEX

SCRIPTURE INDEX

Praise for *Entertaining Angels: Hospitality Programs for the Caring Church*
also by Elizabeth Rankin Geitz

"I have an extensive collection of books in the areas of church growth, evangelism, and newcomer ministry. I have placed *Entertaining Angels* in the section reserved for the very best. It should be mandatory reading for those in evangelism and hospitality ministries."

> *The Reverend George Martin*
> *Director, Church Ad Project*

"They [mainline churches] might learn to do better with people who have had the courage to find their way across a sanctuary threshold, often to be turned off by the indifferent and apathetic inside. Geitz would quicken their interest, open doors."

> *Christian Century*

"... as director of a retreat and conference center, I appreciate and welcome Geitz's thoughts (and thoughtfulness, as she often poses as a newcomer herself while writing)."

> *The Living Church*

"... a fascinating examination of the relevant Biblical texts ... effective guidelines for implementing a hospitality program."

> *Education/Liturgy Resources*
> *Episcopal Diocese of North Carolina*

"First and foremost, *Entertaining Angels* is about the theology of ministry to newcomers. It is as much about the *why* of hospitality as the *how*."

> *The Reverend Dr. Margaret Guenther*
> *Author of* Holy Listening *and* Towards Holy Ground

"... a comprehensive book ... if your parish implemented a program welcoming each person as an angel sent by God — your parish would grow."

> *Maryland Church News*
> *Episcopal Diocese of Maryland*

"The author weaves together the church-business connection through biblical insight, sound scholarship, and personal experience. Every business person can benefit from her creative suggestions in the chapter, 'Outreach to the Business Community.'"

> *John G. Heimann, Chairman*
> *Global Financial Institutions Group, Merrill Lynch*

"We are now and will be, using this for evangelism. It emphasizes welcoming and nurturing; we're getting a lot of lay involvement."

> *The Reverend Carl Spatz, Episcopal Diocese of Nevada*
> *Quoted in* Trinity News: The Magazine of Trinity Church in the City of New York.

"... a buoyant book about our ministry as guests and hosts... an eminently practical guide to the mysterious art of welcoming strangers to the glory of God."

> *The Reverend Dr. John T. Koenig*
> *author of* New Testament Hospitality *and* Recovering New Testament Prayer

Printed in the USA
CPSIA information can be obtained
at www.ICGtesting.com
JSHW082211140824
68134JS00014B/565